BOARD & CEO ROLES FOR ACHIEVING ASSOCIATION GOALS

David A. Westman, MBA, CPA, CAE

association management press

WASHINGTON, DC

The author has worked diligently to ensure that all information in this book is accurate as of the time of publication and consistent with standards of good practice in the general management community. As research and practice advance, however, standards may change. For this reason it is recommended that readers evaluate the applicability of any recommendations in light of particular situations and changing standards.

ASAE: The Center for Association Leadership
1575 I Street, NW
Washington, DC 20005-1103
Phone: (202) 626-2723; (888) 950-2723 outside metropolitan Washington, DC area
Fax: (202) 220-6439
Email: books@asaecenter.org

We connect great ideas and great people to inspire leadership and achievement in the association community.

Keith C. Skillman, CAE, Vice President, Publications, ASAE: The Center for Association Leadership
Baron Williams, CAE, Director of Book Publishing, ASAE: The Center for Association Leadership

Cover and text by Troy Scott Parker, Cimarron Design

This book is available at a special discount when ordered in bulk quantities. For information, contact the ASAE Member Service Center at (202) 371-0940. A complete catalog of titles is available on the ASAE website at www.asaecenter.org.

ISBN-13: 978-0-88034-384-8

Printed in the United States of America.

10 9 8 7 6 5 4 3 2 1

TABLE OF CONTENTS

Appendices 195

TABLE OF EXHIBITS AND APPENDICES

DEDICATION

This book is written for and dedicated to all association board members, aspiring board members, and other member leaders. It is also dedicated to association staff, who put in long hours and in many cases make significant personal sacrifices to serve an association that, in turn, is devoted to advancing a trade or profession.

Finally, it is dedicated to two individuals who have had a profound influence in my life, my engagement in the world of association management, and what success I have enjoyed there. First, to the late John Garde, the well-respected former executive director of the American Association of Nurse Anesthetists from 1983 to 2001. He was my first association client while I was serving as a human resources consultant at KPMG in the early 1990s. His confidence in me and subsequent referrals to his association CEO colleagues helped transform me into an association professional and has led to numerous wonderful experiences as an association CEO and consultant. May he rest in peace!

To my wife and life partner, Lori, who has a Ph.D. in common sense, has served as my primary executive coach for nearly 30 years, and is my biggest cheerleader. She convinced me that I had a book in me that was yearning to be written and that I was in the right place in my career to put the pen to paper. Lori also served as a valued editor, making this book far more readable than it would otherwise be. The process of reflecting on my own accumulated experiences and drawing on the experiences of colleague CEOs has been stimulating and enjoyable. I'm hopeful the result will be helpful to the association profession and the members who donate their time and money in support of individual organizations.

ACKNOWLEDGMENTS

The association world is filled with staff leaders who have made associations their career, in many instances foregoing more lucrative career paths available to them. I want to specifically acknowledge the seasoned veterans listed below. Many of them are Certified Association Executives, and each one graciously responded to my requests for input and feedback regarding this book. Their contributions significantly enhanced the definition of concerns affecting member value and gave me helpful examples to draw on. They also vetted the solutions that I offered, challenging me appropriately, and offering ideas that I had not previously thought of. So, hats off to:

- Mary Alexander, MA, RN, CRNI, FAAN, CAE
- John D. Barnes
- Beth Bernardi, MBA
- Patricia Blake, FASAE, CAE
- Deborah J. Bowen, FACHE, FASAE, CAE
- Kerwin Brown, CAE
- Stacy Brungardt, CAE
- Jill Christie
- Tom Dailly
- Dr. Ron DeHaven, DVM, MBA
- Pierre Désy, MPH, CAE
- Thomas C. Dolan, PhD, FACHE, FASAE, CAE
- Mark T. Engle, DM, FASAE, CAE
- Abe Eshkenazi, CSCP, CPA, FASAE, CAE
- Dave Fellers, FASAE, CAE
- Jefferson C. Glassie, FASAE
- Paula Cozzi Goedert
- Mark J. Golden, FASAE, CAE
- Lynne Thomas Gordon, MBA, RHIA, FACHE, FAHMIA, CAE
- John H. Graham, IV, FASAE, CAE
- Linda Groah MSN, RN, CNOR, NEA-BC, FAAN
- Scott A. Herceg, CAE
- Jerald A. Jacobs
- Gary A. LaBranche, FASAE, CAE
- Lorraine Lavet, MBA
- Christopher E. Laxton, CAE

- Stephen Lieber, CAE
- Elizabeth M. Lucas, MBA, CAE
- J.C. (Chris) Mahaffey, MS, FASAE, CAE
- Jed R. Mandel
- Paul A. Markowski, CAE
- Thomas Marshall
- David J. Martin, CAE
- Christine W. McEntee, MHA, FASAE
- Denny McGuirk
- Ronald S. Moen, MS
- Robert Nelson, CAE
- Peter J. O'Neil, FASAE, CAE
- Wendy Pangburn, MBA, CAE
- Leonard Pfeiffer, MBA
- Michael Anthony Phipps
- Arlene A. Pietranton, PhD, FASAE, CAE
- Helen Pollard, CMP
- Paul Pomerantz, FASAE, CAE
- Cheryl Ronk, CMP, FASAE, CAE
- Edward Salek, CAE
- Robert G. Stein, MBA, FASAE, CAE
- John Thorner, JD, CAE
- Martin B. Tirado, CAE
- Robert T. Van Hook, FASAE, CAE
- Kayla Westman, MSL, CMP
- Dean Wilkerson, JD, MBA, CAE
- James S. Wilson, Jr.
- Richard Yep, FASAE, CAE
- James Zaniello

INTRODUCTION

Our family has a Cavalier King Charles Spaniel named Teddy Bear—Theodore when he's naughty. Teddy is a wonderful, beloved dog who brings us immeasurable joy. However, he does have his idiosyncrasies, most notably when he goes on his daily walk. In spite of attending many doggie obedience schools and learning most tricks with flying colors, Teddy never learned how to heel. When the door flies open, Teddy bounds outside and begins his walk full of energy. He darts continually from one side to the other in a zigzag pattern. Occasionally he pulls way ahead on his leash or alternatively lags far behind to catch one last sniff of a twig.

The dog that starts as a bundle of continual motion quickly becomes tuckered out, as he covers the equivalent of six or seven miles to reach the same destination that his master reached in one mile. His head now droops downward. His tongue starts to hang out and he begins to pant. Yet the zigzagging continues, albeit at a slower pace. Eventually Teddy's eyes say it all. It is time for his middle-aged, not-in-the-best-shape handler to stoop down, pick him up, and carry him the rest of the way home.

Our experiences with Teddy mirror to a large extent the story of many associations. Associations enjoy many advantages compared to their competitors in the for-profit world and elsewhere. But similar to Teddy's inability to heel, many associations' biggest Achilles heel (pardon the pun) is their leadership and governance.

Why is that the case? There are several root causes. Association governance is typically far more complex than other industries. Associations usually have numerous governance entities and a comparably large number of individuals who participate in the governance structure. Most board chairs and other officers serve one-year terms, creating a constant churn in leadership. Each leader has his or her own style, and priorities for the association's direction may also vary from one leader to the next. In addition, by virtue of their daily job roles, board members in associations representing occupations below the C-suite may or may not be naturals at fulfilling the leadership responsibilities of the board of a complex association.

These factors collectively make association leadership extremely challenging for those participating in the governance structure and the staff who support them. The result, equivalent to Teddy's walks, is zigzag leadership. Associations end up consuming far more resources and take much longer to get to the same destination than they need to. Many association leaders become as exhausted as Teddy, but unfortunately, there is not always someone to pick them up and carry them the rest of the way.

In the past, associations did not pay a price for inefficiency and slow progress in serving members. However, it is a new world in the association community! As stated by Harrison Coerver and Mary Byers in *Race for Relevance,* until recently membership in associations has "been more of an obligation, a duty, something you just did, no questions asked."

Associations no longer have a near-monopoly on educational resources, networking opportunities, or even the ability to advocate effectively. Alternative providers are proliferating in the corporate world, and the internet is increasingly serving many of the original purposes of associations. Most associations can no longer hide their shortcomings and flaws behind the generous contributions of corporate sponsors, exhibitors, and advertisers. These entities are increasingly scrutinizing and frequently pulling back financial support as they face pressure from their shareholders to justify such expenditures.

To ensure continuing relevancy, associations need to be nimble, at the top of their game both strategically and operationally, and clearly focused on serving their members. Associations also need the best possible leaders within both the governance structure and staff organization. They need leaders who:

- Are prepared to serve in their roles;
- Understand how best to leverage each other's competencies;
- Are clearly attuned to their fiduciary duties;
- Know how to think and act strategically;
- Can take advantage of the unique strengths associated with their organization;
- Identify and incorporate best practices undertaken by other organizations; and
- Are focused on building member value.

More attention should be focused on these and other leadership attributes in the association world. Member and staff leaders need to continuously consider and decide what they should start doing, stop doing, and do better in their roles, prioritizing, and incorporating these considerations and decisions into progressive action to ensure long-term success for the organization. Absent such attention, association leaders can collectively stand as huge roadblocks to building member value, increasing an organization's nimbleness, making better decisions, and spending the organization's resources wisely.

A plethora of thought leaders and publications address leadership generically. However, relatively few tailor advice to what association leaders need to hear. That is a key purpose of this book—to bridge the gap.

Even more importantly, this book was written to provide guidance on the crucial interplay between an association's board and staff—focusing on the critical CEO/board chair working relationship and the importance of partnering to best serve an association's members. The board/staff dynamic is far more challenging in the association world than in most other industries, primarily because of the temptation board members may feel to involve themselves in responsibilities better fulfilled by staff. Finding the right balance between what the board and staff focus on is crucial to success.

In addressing these two purposes, this book takes the approach of valuing intentional leadership—digging deep into the nitty gritty to create a detailed roadmap for success. To some, this may appear overwhelming and excessively heavy on process. Indeed, there is much to chew on here, even for leaders representing the best run associations. All the more so if you represent a small association and/or one with limited resources.

However, the recommendations that follow have all been battle-tested. I hope they will be viewed by the intended audience—current and aspiring association officers, board and committee members, and the staff who support them—as practical, achievable, and effective in providing the best service and value to members.

The key is to prioritize and not to be discouraged. Rome was not built in a day! Focus on three to five recommendations that you perceive will give your association the best return on the time and resources you have. Once those recommendations have been addressed, you can move on to others in your journey of continuous improvement.

What is the payoff? Anything you start doing, stop doing, or do differently will serve to increase your satisfaction in serving as an association leader—reducing frustration associated with being part of a previously inefficient or dysfunctional organization while building pride in what your association is capable of in the future.

By addressing leadership challenges, your association will also become better positioned to take advantage of what is arguably its most critical asset. Associations have an abundance of passionate, talented members who want to contribute to the organization's success for a variety of reasons. Under sound leadership direction, the wealth of these members' accumulated knowledge, expertise, and free labor can represent a phenomenal resource—a huge competitive advantage that cannot be matched in the for-profit world.

SECTION 1

Setting the Stage for Effective Leadership

CHAPTER 1

Maximize Member Leader Competency

ASSOCIATION GOVERNANCE—SO COMPLICATED COMPARED TO the for-profit world and other industries! So many distinct entities! So many people involved in houses of delegates, boards of directors, committees, and work teams!

It is easy to criticize the structure of governance as an impediment to organizational success, and many authors and consultants have done so. Some have advocated incremental changes, and others, including Coerver and Byers, have recommended such radical changes as a five-member governing board and committees chaired by staff instead of member leaders.

Research conducted by Beth Gazley, PhD and Ashley Bowers, and sponsored by the ASAE Foundation resulting in the publication *What Makes High-Performing Boards* identified a sweet spot for board size—a range for the number of board members for organizations with effective governance practices. The research also revealed that board focus trumps size. Ideally, most associations will heed the advice and migrate, even if only gradually, in these directions. However, it is clear that some associations will not be willing to go down these paths in the foreseeable future, no matter how compelling the case for change might be. Simply put, it is human nature for most of us to fight to the death any attempts to give up power or perquisites that we have attained over years of hard work and, in many cases, personal sacrifice. Fighting such tendencies requires courage and a willingness to forego personal satisfaction for the good of the organization.

I have fought the good fight against human nature with several associations I served as a CEO and consultant. In two specific cases that come to mind, my colleagues (staff in one instance and consulting associates in another) spent hundreds of hours building solid business cases for decreasing the size of the organization's house of delegates—more than 900 delegates for one association and more than 400 for the other. In both instances, we accumulated feedback from members, the preponderance of which clearly demonstrated the desire for a smaller delegate contingent. We likewise presented a solid financial case for change—demonstrating the significant expense associated with a large delegation and how funds could be redirected for more strategic purposes. We even had association benchmarking data to demonstrate how much larger than their peer associations each of these houses were. In spite of all the data, in spite of member preferences, in the end one association opted for no change and the other for only a partial reduction in the delegate count.

By no means do I advocate that association leaders and consultants give up on pursuing changes that result in streamlined governance structures and a lower cost of governance. After all, there have been recent successes in this regard, including the American Nurses Association's decision in 2012 to eliminate its house of delegates. However, political practicalities may delay significant changes for many years, if not decades. In the meantime, associations can at least significantly enhance what they have now by helping their member leaders become far more effective in their roles. Maximizing their effectiveness will ultimately better serve all association members.

For the Good of the Members

The key to maximizing member leader effectiveness is a comprehensive, throughout-the-year performance management program geared towards officers, board members, and committee leaders. In my experience, the need for such a program is far greater in the association world than in corporate America, because association leaders are typically less prepared to undertake their roles than their corporate counterparts. They most likely are not from the C-suite (e.g., CEOs and CFOs) of other successful organizations or luminaries or consultants who have experience leading organizations and serving in board capacities.

They are doctors, nurses, librarians, engineers, accountants, technicians, scientists, or administrative professionals. Some have never been in a supervisory role. Others may have managed a functional area or department, with a few select ones leading an organization. But rarely have they ever previously played a leadership role in anything close to the multimillion-dollar, multifaceted organization that now entrusts them with fiduciary oversight.

Start Training Leaders Before They Begin Their Service

Many associations rely on nominating committees to narrow down the field in selecting future board members and officers, and perhaps the incoming board chair or a committee to select committee chairs and members. In other associations, the culture dictates that any member, with few restrictions, is eligible to be voted by his or her peers into a leadership capacity.

Regardless of how leaders are selected, candidates should be required to demonstrate a minimum understanding of the organization and the related fiduciary responsibilities associated with leadership roles. This can be accomplished through accumulating and disseminating to leadership candidates sets of key documents that are critical for effective performance. There should be a continuum, with lower expectations for committee chair candidates than board member candidates, with the most expectations associated with officer candidates. As an example, required-reading documents for board member candidates could include the association's bylaws, strategic plan, annual report, and perhaps a high level summary of the most recent annual budget and actual results.

At a minimum, candidates should formally attest, with their written or electronic signature, that they have read these documents. Ideally, especially in associations that have few or no restrictions on who can run for office (i.e., no slating of candidates by a nominations committee), candidates should be required to take and pass a test of their knowledge prior to being certified as a candidate for the role they are aspiring to fulfill. This will help separate the wheat from the chaff.

Provide Effective Orientation

Orientation should begin immediately upon election or selection of leaders, before they officially take office. Assuming there is a comprehensive orientation manual (see Appendix 1.1 for a template of topics that should be considered), incoming leaders should be given access to a subset of documents that are critical for them to know from Day 1, expanding upon the set of documents disseminated to them as candidates. Such documentation could, for example, include recent board meeting agendas and minutes, among other things.

Similar to the procedure for candidates, new leaders should attest prior to taking office that their pre-reading assignment has been completed. In addition, it would be helpful for the new leaders to observe or attend telephonically one or more meetings of the board or committee they will be serving on, so they can obtain a sense of the dynamics and typical participant interactions.

An in-person orientation, supplementing the manual, should occur before or at the first meeting associated with the new leaders' terms of office. Ideally, a portion of the orientation experience will include only the new members–led by a team of individuals including, but not necessarily limited to, the board chair and/or chair-elect, the CEO, and legal counsel. A template agenda for such an orientation is included as Appendix 1.2. A second portion of the orientation should include all board members. It should serve as a team-building experience and reinforce for the veterans key concepts that may have been forgotten since their own orientation experiences.

The chair, chair-elect, treasurer, and other officers should receive special, individualized orientations. For each one, this should include a detailed discussion of her/his fiduciary role, responsibilities, and the types of interactions they can expect to have with other officers, board and committee members, external stakeholders (e.g., the auditing firm in the case of the treasurer), and staff. Perhaps most important, they need to have a grasp on the commitments and expectations they will be asked to fulfill during their tenure, ideally laid out on a monthly calendar.

If time and budget permit, it is highly beneficial for the incoming chair and/or chair-elect to attend an external orientation program, with the CEO, which is specifically targeted at such positions. For example, the American Society of Association Executives (ASAE) offers a highly recommended CEO Symposium for chief elected and chief executive officers. Such programs provide opportunities for these two critical leaders to connect, define priorities, and determine how best to work together.

Tap Into Your Best Current Leaders as Mentors

Many organizations have found it helpful to institute a mentorship program as a supplement to the formal orientation program. There is only so much that a new member leader can absorb from reading policies, procedures, and other documents relative to the functioning of a board or committee. Mentors help new member leaders feel welcome and integrated into the mainstream of board or committee operations. Perhaps even more important, they can provide a wealth of information about the informal practices, the cultural dos and don'ts, and unwritten expectations. New member leaders' effectiveness depends in large part on how quickly they can get pick up on these nuances.

Mentors should be well-respected (but not necessarily the longest tenured members of the governance entity associated with the new leader) and should be familiar and comfortable with the operation, programs, and culture of the entity. They should be generally acknowledged as supportive, positive, and truthful. It is helpful if the mentor and mentee have similar interests and experiences. Mentors should commit to being available via phone or email while serving in the role.

The ideal mentor will:

- Assure that the mentee is introduced to others and integrated at meetings, meals, social settings, and other interactions.
- Initiate and encourage ongoing communication in addition to regularly scheduled meetings and teleconferences of the governance entity.
- Convey information regarding the entity's traditions and unwritten rules.
- Ensure that the mentee understands all assignments, responsibilities, and deadlines.
- Be approachable as the go-to person for any and all questions posed by the mentee.
- Make the mentee aware of relevant meetings and social events he or she should attend.
- Augment the organization's formal orientation relative to administrative procedures, including questions about travel arrangements, expense reports, meeting reports, and staff contacts.
- Assist the mentee in understanding and obtaining key resources and using them, including online templates for reports.
- Act as a sounding board for new ideas and how to effectively communicate them to others.

Mentors themselves should be subject to performance feedback. There should be a mid-year check-in with each mentor and mentee to ensure that the working relationship is viewed as positive and effective. If such is not the case, a switch in mentors may be needed. At the end of the year, both individuals should be debriefed to understand what went well, what did not go well, and what lessons were learned for future mentor/mentee relationships.

Educate Beyond Orientation

Even the best orientation and mentor programs will take association member leaders only so far in terms of helping them be effective in their roles. Much of what is initially learned through orientation will be forgotten over time and should be periodically reinforced. There will also be additional important topics to address that cannot be squeezed into already packed orientation agendas. Therefore, associations should consider allotting at least 30 minutes, and ideally more time, at each meeting for board education. Alternatively, the education can be accomplished via archived webinars or other approaches between meetings.

Similar to curriculum development in any setting, the process should start with a needs assessment. The board officers and CEO certainly will have a sense of the board's strengths and weaknesses based on what they see occurring. Year-end board surveys can also provide guidance. However, perhaps the best gauge of educational needs can come from the board members themselves.

Appendix 1.3 includes a set of competencies and skills that are typically important for board members to master if they are to be effective. Each board member should be asked to indicate which of these competencies and skills represent strengths or weaknesses. The collective input from all board members should be used to guide prioritization of topics to address first in board member continuing education.

In many instances staff can serve as faculty for specific topics (e.g., helping the board gain a better understanding of core functional areas such as corporate development and member service). In other instances a past or current member leader may have the requisite expertise to serve as faculty. If the budget allows, outside speakers can be engaged to attend board meetings in person or via webcast.

Following is an example annual curriculum pertaining to board education. Several of the example topics purposely include a blend of education and strategic thinking, which can subsequently be helpful when the association undertakes strategic planning:

Board Meeting 1: Interpretation and review of the association's financial statements.

Board Meeting 2: Decision-making authority and parameters for the board, committees, and staff.

Board Meeting 3: The future of educational technology and its impact on the association.

Board Meeting 4: The board's fiduciary role relative to risk management.

Board Meeting 5: Current status and future opportunities relative to collaborating with other organizations.

A final note about ongoing board education: It can be helpful to use a blend of techniques to convey and ingrain key points in the minds of session participants. One frequently overlooked technique is the use of case studies or hypothetical scenarios. In one organization I worked with, a consultant was engaged to create a series of case studies addressing issues that frequently arise in the association world. These became a component of subsequent board education over a period of years. Following are synopses of two such case studies that address board and staff role definition and decision-making parameters:

Case Study 1: The CEO has received an unexpected opportunity to partner with another association on a series of conferences that are applicable to both your organization and the other association. Is teaming with this association an operational decision to be made by the CEO or a strategic decision that requires board input and/or approval? If the latter, what is the appropriate division of accountability for the staff and board?

Case Study 2: The CEO has made the decision to reassign a long-term employee from one department to another. This employee is well liked by the board, is angry about the proposed change, and has vocalized her concerns to staff colleagues and selected board members who she considers to be friends. What should the response of board members be when they are approached by an angry employee regarding this or other human resources-related actions taken by the CEO? What role, if any, does the board have relative to human resource management within the staff organization?

Discussions from such case studies can become quite lively, with many "ah-ha" moments on the part of those participating in the process. Perhaps most important, such case studies can promote mutual understanding of organizational roles, leading to better governance and, ultimately, service to the members.

Assess Entity and Individual Leader Performance

Even if you have the ideal approach for vetting candidates for leadership positions, your orientation process is sound, you facilitate mentoring, and your program of continuing leader education is robust, there is no guarantee that solid performance will follow. That is why ongoing assessment is so important.

Assessment can and should take several forms. Many associations have found value in undertaking brief assessments at the end of each board and committee meeting. These assessments not only provide input on participants' educational needs but also can result in helpful insights on the overall effective and efficient functioning of the governance entity. Exhibit 1.1 provides an assessment instrument template that has been used by boards with whom I have worked. The chair typically receives helpful and frequently surprising feedback relative to her/his facilitation skills. Feedback also can identify needs for coaching individual meeting participants about how they can be more effective and perceived better by their colleagues. This can serve to nip problems in the bud before they become serious issues and drain on leader and staff time.

It is also important to undertake year-end assessments of the board and committees as entities, as well as individual members. Such assessments can and should be used to:

- Narrow down education priorities for the following year, leading to a curriculum of group education for the board or committee.
- Identify coaching opportunities at the individual level.
- Influence future assignments of governance roles for committee chairs and liaison roles to various external organizations.

Effective assessment methodologies and tools pertaining to nonprofit governance entities are readily available. For example, BoardSource, in partnership with the American Society of Association Executives, offers an association-specific Board Self-Assessment survey, which gathers feedback from individual board members and measures the collective performance of the board. It also offers a peer-to-peer survey, which asks board members to evaluate their individual performance and that of peers. Survey results provide useful perceptions of the board's performance and culture and reveal how both are affected by the style and engagement of its individual members.

And the Buck Stops With...

In most situations, CEOs of associations carry final accountability similar to their counterparts in the corporate world. The CEO should have:

- The ability to craft and administer officer, board, and committee orientation programs;
- Responsibility for preparing and administering a curriculum of continuing board member education;

Exhibit 1.1

Board Meeting Assessment Survey

Questions	Yes	Somewhat Agree	No	Suggestions for Improvement
The agenda was clear, supported by the necessary documents, and circulated prior to the meeting.				
All board members were prepared to discuss materials sent in advance.				
Reports were clear and contained needed information.				
We avoided getting into administrative management or operational details.				
A diversity of opinions was expressed and issues were dealt with in a respectful manner.				
Decisions were made in the best interests of the organization and its members and not based on personal perspectives.				
The chair guided the meeting effectively.				
Board members were engaged (minimal multitasking) and participated responsibly during the meeting.				
Next steps were identified and responsibilities assigned.				
The meeting began and ended on time.				
The meeting room was conducive to work.				
We enjoyed being together.				

What did you most appreciate about the meeting relative to its facilitation, participant interactions, and results?

___

___

What additional comments or suggestions do you have to improve the effectiveness and efficiency of our meetings?

___

___

• • •

- Responsibility for coordinating board and individual member performance assessment; and
- Competency relative to ongoing governance administration, serving as a coach to board officers.

The CEO and other staff supporting the governance function should also be charged with being attuned to best practices in board and committee operations through involvement in their own professional associations. They can use this knowledge, along with their first-hand experiences of what has worked and has not worked over time with the association, to propose changes in the governance structure and operations.

Member leaders certainly play key roles in assuring competence within the board and committee structure. The chair and other officers should be consulted in annual fine-tuning of the orientation process and manual, approve the curriculum of ongoing education, serve as faculty for selected orientation program topics, and provide other input.

It may also be helpful to establish and assign the role of governance coach to the immediate past chair. This can become a meaningful, influential role for a position that is typically underused in many organizations. In this capacity, he/she could provide input to the CEO regarding design and implementation of the various components of leader development outlined in this chapter.

The governance coach will ideally take the lead in summarizing and conveying to board and committee colleagues results from formal assessment processes of governance entities and their individual members. Doing so will shield the CEO from potential charges of favoritism and political bias.

Perhaps most important, the governance coach is better positioned than staff to serve as the primary coach to individual board members whose bad behaviors or poor performance are detrimental to effective organizational governance. Such members are much more likely to accept and respond positively to such feedback and accompanying suggestions from a respected peer.

Tying It Back to the Members

The more competent and engaged board and committee members are the more likely their involvement will serve to advance the interests of the association and its members. More member leader attention will be devoted to their key fiduciary responsibilities and hopefully less attention to operational issues that should be the purview of staff. Meetings of various governance entities will be run more efficiently, which may serve to reduce the number of meetings and the time spent in them; this will ultimately decrease the cost of governance. Decisions made will likely have more impact and be appropriate, given the decision makers' more solid knowledge of the organization. Less time will be taken during board meetings to address basic questions to which board members should already know the answers.

Perhaps most important, when an organization demonstrates a commitment to develop the competence of its member leaders and make the best use of their time, it is more likely to attract the type of high caliber candidates to board and committee roles that the organization needs. "Dead wood" leaders will be gradually weeded out and replaced by those who are there for the right reasons.

CHAPTER 2

Assign Roles to Those Best Suited

OTHER THAN INDIVIDUALS WHO SERVE in the governance structure or work as staff for an association, few people can comprehend how unclear and ever-changing role assignments and decision making can be in the association world. The governance structure in almost every other industry includes officers, a board, and a handful of committees. The individuals serving in leadership capacities typically do so for a period of many years, providing a level of continuity and historical perspective that makes role definition and decision making parameters relatively straightforward.

How different it is for associations! The similarities with other industries end with the presence of officers and a board. Some professional societies have a house of delegates that frequently battles with the board for decision making authority and future strategic direction of the association. (See more about strategic direction in Chapter 6.) Associations also typically have four, five, or more times the number of committees and work teams than other types of organizations, except perhaps the not-to-be-emulated models of federal and state governments. The leaders of each association governance entity understandably want something worthwhile to do and the opportunity to make decisions and influence the association's success.

A further complication for association management is the lack of leadership continuity. Key officers such as the chair and treasurer typically serve only one-year terms. A third or more of many association board members turn over annually, and committee chairs and members frequently serve only one- or two-year terms. Consequently, it is much more difficult to rely on oral historical perspectives of long-tenured leaders to ensure consistency regarding "how things are done here."

All these factors present challenges in terms of who does what. Changing expectations, personalities, and in some cases the political power of those occupying the positions of chair, treasurer, and committee chairs can result in wide swings of authority and decision making assignments from year to year. The resulting confusion and turf battles serve to delay or end progress on strategic and operational initiatives—to the detriment of the organization and its members.

The lack of clarity and consistency in role definition and decision making accountability can negatively affect staff relations. Depending on who the chair and other key leaders are, the role of the CEO and staff can change 180 degrees from one year to the next. One year the CEO is viewed as a true association leader, with accountability for decision making similar to what is given to a bank or manufacturing CEO. The next year he or she is relegated to the status of manager—better seen and not heard—primarily responsible for implementing decisions made within the governance structure. The organizational whiplash this causes, as well as frustration and poor morale within the organization's staff, results in unhealthy staff turnover. It also typically leads to diminished productivity on the parts of staff that remain—again to the detriment of the organization and its members.

As an association CEO who served 12 different bosses (chairs) in 10 years and as a consultant to many other associations, I have experienced firsthand the effects of poor role definition, accountability assignments, and decision making involving governance entities and staff. But associations are not lost causes. If the collective mindsets of member leaders and staff are aligned, and with appropriate processes and tools, associations can rise above the challenges just mentioned. Even the operations of large, complex governance structures can be streamlined, enabling associations to compete effectively and increase member value.

For the Good of the Members

The appropriate mindset for member and staff leaders to have relative to role and decision-making assignments is to ensure that the best interests of the organization and its members are kept in the forefront. There must be a commitment to make assignments to the individuals and entities that are best positioned by expertise, experience, time, and other resources to make the best decisions and effectively implement them. Assignments should not be made as a reward or perquisite in recognition of an individual's past service to the organization or because of pressure that is levied on the chair or CEO to give an individual or committee a decision-making role.

It is certainly difficult and it can take political courage to shift to such a mindset when historical precedent dictates otherwise. But hopefully some of the upcoming horror stories will help convince those reticent to make the shift in thinking. The following process steps and tools can be used to optimize role assignments and decision-making accountability.

Identify Typical Decisions You Need to Make

It is impossible to anticipate every decision that needs to be made during the course of an organization's history. However, many decisions must be made on a recurring basis—annually, monthly, or even more frequently. The articulation of these decisions, along with accountability assignments, can serve as a helpful guide for decision making when the need for unusual, impossible-to-anticipate decisions arises.

Following are just a few of the key decisions most associations routinely face at the officer, board, and CEO levels. As you reflect on your own organization, is there clarity regarding which positions and entities are accountable for making them? Are there additional situations where there is confusion regarding who the decision maker is or are there situations where the decision-making position or entity changes too frequently?

Strategy and Policy Role

This includes establishing the organization's vision, mission, and strategic direction; approving the committee structure and charges; and approving major policies.

Decisions:

1. Determine the process for reviewing and revising the strategic plan.
2. Determine what research is needed to support decision making relative to the organization's strategic plan development.
3. Approve and revise the strategic plan.
4. Authorize implementation of specific new products, programs, and services.
5. Approve governance policies.
6. Approve appointments of volunteers to committees and ad hoc work groups.
7. Approve charges for committees and ad hoc work groups.

Positioning and Alignment Role

This includes approving the organization's role and position with regard to governmental legislation/regulations and approving the organization's affiliations, sponsorships, endowments, and other relationships with various outside entities.

Decisions:

1. Approve/reject collaboration requests from other local, national or international organizations.
2. Appoint organizational liaisons for collaboration opportunities.
3. Respond to requests for the organization to send representatives in official capacities.
4. Respond to requests from external organizations for monetary support.
5. Endorse other organizations' programs and activities.
6. Respond to specific advocacy requests, including letters to Congress and regulators.
7. Approve vendor partnerships to jointly sell products or services to members and nonmembers.
8. Approve various forms of corporate support, including grants, sponsorships, member service programs, and advertising.

Accountability Role

This includes approving budgets and major financial transactions, monitoring overall organizational performance and quality of service delivery, managing the CEO's performance, and monitoring compliance with the code of ethics and board policies/procedures.

Decisions—Financial:

1. Approve the organization's investment policy.
2. Approve the annual operating budget.
3. Approve the capital budget.
4. Approve changes in member dues rates.
5. Approve annual meeting participant registration fees.
6. Approve pricing for products, programs, and services.
7. Approve board and committee member expenses.
8. Approve CEO-specific expenses.
9. Approve budget transfers.

10. Approve unbudgeted expenditures, with typically different decision-making parameters depending on the amount.

Decisions—Human Resources Related:

1. Select the CEO.
2. Manage performance of the CEO.
3. Approve and revise the organization's overall compensation strategy.
4. Determine the CEO's and critical staff compensation packages.

Decisions—Other:

1. Revise conflict of interest, confidentiality, intellectual property, and code of conduct agreements.
2. Select and manage the performance of key vendors, including the auditing firm, legal counsel, and consultants.
3. Select and manage the performance of all other vendors.
4. Approve the content of key member communications pieces (e.g., the annual report).

The articulation of decisions can be extended to the committee level, addressing situations where there is confusion or shifting sands regarding where decision-making authority resides. Is the committee chair, committee as a whole, or staff liaison empowered to make decisions?

Assign Roles and Decision-Making Accountability Within the Governance Structure

Once typical decisions have been articulated and categorized, the next step is to assign decision-making authority. Consultants and others offer a variety of tools to help associations assign accountabilities. Exhibit 2.1 is but one example, a single page of a much more comprehensive decision-making matrix. The matrix assigns various financial management roles to the following:

- Association officers;
- The board;
- Key board committees;
- Generically to other committees; and
- The CEO, assuming subsequent delegation to staff in many cases.

In addition to identifying the ultimate decision maker for each decision, there are opportunities to indicate when other individuals or entities need to be involved in making the decision or at least be notified when a decision has been made.

Exhibit 2.1

Organization X Governance Decision-Making Matrix

Role Key

D = Decision maker, I = Involved, N = Notified,
blank = No role independent of decision maker

Accountability Role

Includes approving budgets and other financial transaction, monitoring overall organization performance and quality of service delivery, managing the CEO's performance, and monitoring compliance with the code of ethics and board policies/procedures

Financial Performance Related

Decision	Board Chair	Board Chair-Elect	Secretary	Treasurer	Board	Executive Committee	Finance Committee	Other Committees	CEO	Commentary
Approve and revise the organization's investment policy				I	N		D		I	The Finance Committee reviews and makes decisions pertaining to the organization's investment strategy, led by the treasurer with input from staff and external investment advisors.
Approve the organization's operating budget				I	D		I		I	Staff, in close consultation with the treasurer, prepares the operating budget annually, considering the organization's mission, vision, and strategic plan as well as guidance/parameters outlined by the board (e.g., extent to which a dues increase will be entertained). The Finance Committee approves the draft budget in October and forwards a recommendation for approval to the board, which approves the final budget.
Approve Annual Meeting participant registration fees					N			D	I	The Annual Meeting Committee makes decisions based on benchmarking with other relevant professional societies, budgetary, and other considerations and with input provided by relevant staff.

Decision	Board Chair	Board Chair-Elect	Secretary	Treasurer	Board	Executive Committee	Finance Committee	Other Committees	CEO	Commentary
Manage operating expenses				I	N		I		D	The CEO is accountable to the board for attaining the overall budgeted net income from operations and strategic initiatives. The CEO makes decisions that may lead to overages in certain budget line items, as long as they are offset by under-budget spending in other areas. First the treasurer, and then the Finance Committee reviews and discusses budget variances on a periodic basis with the CFO, and the full board is notified of budget performance through Finance Committee reporting.

Note: This is an example of how you might format a decision-making matrix. Every organization has its own unique set of circumstances and characteristics. The important takeaway is that accountability roles are assigned and everyone understands them. It's not to suggest, for example, that you create an Annual Meeting Committee if your association has staff currently making this decision.

• • •

The last column of the template is important in terms of clarifying the intent and nature of decision making, involvement, and notification assignments. The value of completing this column increases with each passing year, as those responsible for initially creating the matrix rotate out of leadership positions. New organizational leaders, without having the color commentary, may be more inclined to misinterpret or arbitrarily change decision-making roles without giving appropriate consideration to the significant thought and hard work their predecessors undertook in previously defining such roles.

That is not to say that role and decision-making accountabilities should remain cast in stone. Operating environments change over time; organizations grow or contract; and the governance structure itself can change. At a minimum, the decision-making matrix or matrices should be reviewed by the board and CEO biannually, with changes thoroughly communicated to the affected individuals and entities.

The matrix should be recognized as one of the most critical orientation documents an organization has for new board members, other member leaders, and staff leaders. It should be a must-read and the bible in terms of how they interact with each other. The chair and CEO should be jointly responsible to ensure that it is adhered to, especially given the inevitable challenges various individuals with self-serving interests will make to the organization's decision-making accountability assignments.

Ensure the Right Roles Are Assigned to the Right Entities and Individuals

Identifying decisions that need to be made and assigning them to entities and individuals may seem relatively straightforward. However, organizational nimbleness, success in generating more revenue or incurring less expense, and ultimately member value itself, depend heavily on who the decision makers are and the roles assigned to other individuals and entities.

Consider a professional society that has a house of delegates and a board. Officers and members of the two entities are continually at odds about the appropriate future direction of the society as well as the appropriate allocation of the society's financial and time resources to various products, programs, and services.

In this case, the house of delegates, not the board, has the authority to approve annual operating and capital budgets. The house meets once a year for several days, during which budget review, discussion, and approval are just a few of the many items on the agenda. The house members typically represent and devote most of their time and attention to the geographic or special interest constituencies that selected them. They might lack training in or knowledge of budget development and management principles and practices. They may also have only a superficial understanding of the society's strategy, inner workings, and operating constraints.

Aside from the dangers inherent in entrusting an organization's financial future to an entity that lacks time and expertise to undertake the role, the impact goes much further. The Finance Committee, followed by the board, must first vet the budget that is ultimately presented to the house. The budget then needs to be documented, printed, and forwarded to house delegations months in advance of the house meeting, theoretically to give the delegations time to consider it, although in practice that does not always happen. Because of all these process steps, staff needs to start the budget development process nearly two years in advance of the fiscal year.

This is well before there is sufficient knowledge of what the operational environment will look like and the corresponding needs for scarce budgetary dollars.

What ultimately happens? After all the time, hard work, and resources consumed previously, the house can and frequently does vote to approve significant budgetary changes, most often additions benefitting a specific constituency or special interest group, without time for due consideration.

Sound familiar? Think Congress and state legislatures, whose members likewise represent narrow constituencies and frequently add amendments to bills at the last moment without time to digest the consequences. These are not role models for effective decision making.

Keeping in mind the best interests of the organization and its members, the accountability for budget approval should lie with the board. To the extent a house of delegates exists—and that is a whole different topic of conversation—its role should be limited based on what it is best suited for, perhaps approving bylaw amendments and submitting advisory resolutions to the board for its consideration.

This example is not an isolated one. Most long-term association CEOs, if asked, can provide numerous examples of how decision-making accountability assignments have detracted from member value creation and maintenance. Most of these examples relate to an under-reliance on expertise where it exists and a corresponding conveyance of decision-making authority as a reward or perquisite in recognition of an individual's past service to the organization.

Digging a Little Deeper

Inappropriate role assignments tend to be more prevalent in some areas than others, especially pertaining to functional areas within the staff organization. Member leaders readily keep their distance in day-to-day management of the association's accounting, technology, facilities, and other functional areas they are uninterested in or where they readily acknowledge staff expertise.

However, it is a different story if member leaders think they have expertise in a given area. Following are discussions of functional areas that board members tend to meddle in. They are frequently the subjects of moaning, complaining, and brainstorming when groups of association CEOs convene at their own professional association meetings. In each instance, one or more scenarios are presented, followed by suggestions for appropriate role assignments.

Human Resource Management

Outside the association world, it is commonly understood that the CEO is responsible for all decision making relative to staff hiring, development, performance management, remuneration, termination, and other human resource issues, subject to overall constraints imposed by the organization's budget. In some associations, however, board members and other member leaders tend to meddle, influence, and in some cases dictate key human resource management decisions. Note the following real-life example:

> Association X hired a director to lead a programmatic area that was core to the organization's mission and near and dear to most of the board members. The director was highly credentialed in terms of education, experience, and publications. This individual also interacted well with volunteer leaders, many of whom developed friendships with him.
>
> Within the organization's staff, it was an entirely different story. Despite repeated interventions from human resources department staff and the CEO, the director operated in a silo. He refused to collaborate appropriately with other departments in the development of the work product. He made decisions beyond the scope of his assigned accountability. He missed numerous key deadlines for the accomplishment of performance milestones, leaving others to pick up the pieces. Finally, he treated his subordinates poorly.
>
> The CEO faced a dilemma. She knew how highly the director was perceived by board and other member leaders. Yet the chaos the director was causing within the staff was resulting in serious morale problems and jeopardizing the timely and effective rollout of key new products, programs, and services.
>
> The CEO shared these concerns with the officer group along with her intentions to terminate the director if there was not a significant performance turnaround within a specified time. Even though the CEO's employment agreement called for her total authority to make staffing decisions, the officer group collectively dismissed the CEO's concerns and warned her not to terminate the director or face severe consequences herself.
>
> What was the result? The CEO, understanding the board's preferences, initially went against her better judgment, kept the problem director in his role, and experienced continuing and expanding concerns within the staff. Other staff members were aware that the director was not being appropriately disciplined and surmised correctly that he was being protected by the board. The situation deteriorated to the point that nearly two years later the CEO did what should have been done long before—she terminated

the director. As predicted, her action ultimately contributed significantly to her own termination less than a year later.

Similar examples of member leader intervention in human resources management abound. In some associations, individual board members or the board as a whole have attempted to influence hiring decisions, design the staff organizational structure, and be involved in salary and incentive compensation decisions for specific employees.

In all such cases, the authority of the CEO is usurped. This intervention stymies the CEO's ability to drive execution of strategic and operating plans. It can also prevent CEOs from creating the type of internal operational environment and culture that they deem important.

Simply stated, member leaders need to stay clear of human resources management, other than holding the CEO accountable for attaining overall performance targets relative to:

- Strategic plan implementation;
- Budget attainment;
- Member service satisfaction; and perhaps
- Employee turnover rates and overall employee satisfaction.

That said, there are situations when member leaders, if asked by the CEO, can play limited but important HR-related roles. There are other situations where the CEO should notify the board, or at least its officers, of specific staff-related actions that have been taken.

Exhibit 2.2 provides a more detailed articulation of how selected human resource management roles might be handled in an association where member leaders are appropriately focused on governance and the staff on operations. Note that references in the matrix to CEO decision making infers significant delegation to the human resources department head.

Meeting Management

Meetings, most notably annual meetings, are the lifeblood of many associations. They are a key reason why individuals and organizations join associations and a primary source of revenue to support less profitable activities and the overall infrastructure.

Aside from the vast array of educational and networking opportunities offered, the annual meeting is frequently the key venue for an association's member leaders to celebrate their accomplishments. They get to stand in the spotlight in front of hundreds, if not thousands, of colleagues during general sessions and various social events.

Exhibit 2.2

Human Resources Management Role Definition

Role Key

D = Decision maker, I = Involved, and N = Notified

Role	Officers	Board	CEO/Staff	Clarifying Details
Design the staff organization structure		N	D	The CEO determines the appropriate staffing configuration, including design of specific job roles and reporting relationships, based on attaining the strategic direction established by the board.
Select/hire director level positions	I		D	The CEO may, at his discretion, involve the officers in vetting final candidates for selected positions, especially for roles that are mission-specific or require extensive knowledge of the trade or profession.
Select/hire remaining staff		N	D	The CEO has sole responsibility for recruiting and selecting all remaining staff to fill vacant positions. The board will be notified of new hires at the manager level and higher no later than the new employee's start date.
Manage staff performance, including disciplinary measures associated with director-level and above staff	I/N		D	The board sets performance expectations/metrics for the organization to attain as part of approving the strategic plan, and in the course of establishing annual performance metrics for the CEO. The CEO determines how these expectations and metrics will be delivered (e.g., product development, marketing, utilization of technology) and manages functional performance accordingly. The CEO will seek feedback on key contractor and departmental performance as part of the year-end board survey process. Results will be used to manage performance. The CEO will notify the chair of significant performance concerns and disciplinary actions pertaining to director level and above staff (i.e., those involving issuance of a written warning) as soon as the need for such action has been determined and may elicit the chair's input on how best to address concerns.
Terminate staff		N	D	Termination of any staff member at the manager level and up will be announced to the full board no later than the date an employee separates from the organization.

Role	Officers	Board	CEO/Staff	Clarifying Details
Select and manage performance of the CEO, including disciplinary or termination decisions	D	I	I	The board as a whole determines the specific methodology and performance assessment instruments that will be utilized in any given year. The chair coordinates the mid-year and year-end performance assessment processes, ensuring input has been sought from all relevant stakeholders and considered. The officer group assesses the CEO's performance at mid-year. All board members provide input regarding the CEO's year-end performance. The board also collectively finalizes CEO performance metrics within the first 90 days of any given fiscal year. At least tri-annually, the CEO will be subject to a 360 degree feedback process, the results of which will be conveyed to the chair as input for the CEO's performance assessment. The CEO provides input into development of performance metrics and completes performance self-assessments at both mid-year and year-end.
Approve/ revise the organization's compensation strategy		I	D	The board has decision-making authority relative to the overall staff compensation budget. However, the CEO makes decisions regarding specific strategies and administration pertaining to compensation components (i.e., base salary administration, incentive compensation, traditional and non-traditional benefits). The CEO reviews and potentially revises the compensation strategy annually with input from the board. The strategy document is included as a component of board orientation.

• • •

Such acknowledgement is appropriate, given the years of commitment and personal sacrifice that frequently go hand-in-hand with becoming an association leader. However, in many cases an accompanying entitlement mentality bleeds over. Leaders adopt a mindset that the annual meeting is their party to do with as they please, regardless of the best interests of members and the association itself.

Note the following two scenarios:

Scenario 1: Association Y, similar to many associations, had a very rigorous, well-defined process for selecting future annual meeting destinations.

Potential cities and venues were assessed and prioritized based on criteria that included financial considerations, air lift, quality of accommodations, and member appeal. After more than six months of work on the part of the Annual Meeting Committee (AMC) and staff as well as substantial back-and-forth negotiations with finalist city representatives, the AMC chair was ready to present the committee's recommendation to the board.

The board chair had a different idea. He lived in a large city that was physically capable of hosting the annual meeting. However, it was a city viewed by the association's members, validated by member survey data, as one of the least attractive cities in the country.

The chair, using his stature and political power to the utmost, literally coerced his board colleagues into rejecting the AMC's recommendation and instead select his preferred city. This was accomplished without due consideration by the board of member input and how the city rated on the site selection criteria.

What was the result? The association's marketing department doubled its budget and the time they spent promoting the meeting because of concerns about meeting attendance. Nevertheless, attendance at the meeting was down by nearly 50 percent from the prior year. This translated into almost $500,000 less net revenue from the meeting than the prior year and put the organization into extreme belt-tightening mode. It eliminated or diminished funding for key strategic initiatives that would have benefited the members.

Scenario 2: In Association Z there was a long-standing tradition of member leaders approving menu selection for all meals, breaks, and social events as part of the budgeting process. Each year meeting management staff professionals investigated options for menus. They used data regarding popular and unpopular food and beverage items from previous events, negotiated well, and ultimately presented their recommendations to the AMC. The AMC, typically supporting the personal preferences of one or two vocal members, almost always pushed back, adding high-priced items to menus that had questionable appeal to most attendees.

One year, with the association experiencing financial challenges, it was clear that any additional menu items proposed by the AMC had to be accompanied by reductions elsewhere in order to meet overall budget targets. One AMC member expressed a desire to add hard-boiled eggs to all breakfast menus, which at that time were priced at $3.50 each. To cut expenses elsewhere, the AMC directed meetings department staff, despite their objections, to eliminate coffee service during some breaks and reduce quantities ordered for other breaks.

This change led to significant member backlash. Most of the eggs went uneaten. Scores of members were visibly upset and complained about the lack of coffee on site. Meetings staff was forced to order additional coffee on site at inflated prices in spite of the budgetary implications.

Even with these last-minute actions, numerous meeting attendees expressed their dissatisfaction on the subsequent meeting satisfaction survey, conveying their belief that the association was nickel-and-diming them. This diminished their satisfaction with the overall meeting. All of this was the result of a single committee member's desire for hard boiled eggs!

Meeting management, from site selection to menu selection and everything in between, is highly complex. There are opportunities for huge swings in overall profitability—or lack thereof—depending on decisions that are made months, and in some cases years, before events take place. Given the importance of these decisions on an association's overall financial health as well as member satisfaction, member leaders in most instances need to "back off." They need to let staff meeting professionals do the job they were hired to do. These individuals, many of whom have graduated from meeting management degree programs and/or are Certified Meeting Professionals (CMP), have the combination of skills and experiences to create the best participant experience with the best financial return to the organization.

The board and other member leaders instead need to focus on and hold staff accountable for attaining budgeted attendance and financial results and ensuring participant satisfaction with the annual meeting and other events.

Exhibit 2.3 provides a more detailed articulation of how selected meeting management roles might be handled in an association where member leaders are appropriately focused on governance and the staff on operations. Note that references in the matrix to CEO decision making infers significant delegation to the meetings department head.

Marketing Management

Many people think they're good at marketing. Board and committee members sometimes get down in the weeds, dictating to staff how the annual meeting and other key products, programs, and services will be priced and promoted. In some associations, member leaders even write or approve specific content appearing in collateral pieces and dictate the frequency that marketing emails and other communications are sent to members.

In some associations marketing decisions are treated as a perk of office. The chair or another designated member leader is given complete latitude

Exhibit 2.3

Meeting Management Role Definition

Role Key

D = Decision maker, I = Involved, and N = Notified

Role	Officers	Board	Board Committee (if applicable)	CEO/Staff	Clarifying Details
Select sites for the annual meeting and other events		N	I	D	Assuming there is an Annual Meeting Committee (AMC) or equivalent, this entity will collaborate with staff to define criteria that will be utilized in selecting meeting destinations, ideally considering member survey and other relevant data. This could include specifying regions within or outside of the United States where the meeting could be held. Within these parameters, staff will research specific destinations, select the best option, and notify the board. Notification will include an indication of why/how the choice best met the selection criteria.
Establish budgets for the annual meeting and all its components		D	I	I	The AMC will provide input relative to events and other meeting components that should be budgeted within the overall annual meeting program, along with the desired member experience (i.e., quality) that should be targeted. Staff will then prepare budgets in line with these parameters, which will be vetted by the AMC and subsequently approved by the board.
Negotiate contracts for all meeting-related facilities and services		N	I	D	All contract negotiations will be undertaken by staff based on specifications developed with AMC input. Staff will convey selected details of negotiated contracts to the board.
Finalize specific locations, rooms, and configurations for educational and social events	I		I	D	The AMC will be consulted regarding these issues, along with all staff departments affected by needs for space. The board chair and other officers will be consulted specifically with regard to events that they host. However, the meetings department will be charged with finalizing room selection and configuration for all events.

Role	Officers	Board	Board Committee (if applicable)	CEO/Staff	Clarifying Details
Finalize menu selection (food and beverage) for all meals and social events			I	D	The AMC will establish broad parameters relative to menu selection, including budget limits per meal and the preferred cuisine for social events. Meetings department staff will operate within these parameters to finalize specific menu items.

• • •

to select or even personally design graphics that will appear on the annual meeting program cover or other key marketing pieces.

Marketing decision roles also extend to the website, a crucial marketing channel for all associations. The website's homepage is the association's first and most important impression with members, prospective members, other key stakeholders, and the general public. It is imperative that the homepage be welcoming and easy to navigate. It should entice the visitor to drill down further into the website to pages that provide more information and to engage with your association and its products, programs, and services.

It is critical that the homepage provides only the items of utmost importance at a specific point in time. Unfortunately, the homepage can instead become a bulletin board for everything the association is doing. This is especially true when member leaders perceive their particular pet project or piece of information is of critical importance. Note the following case study:

> At Association M numerous board members continually demanded that specific items be promoted on the home page, along with a plethora of direct links. An already busy homepage became a cluttered mess, making navigation increasingly difficult for users, with nothing standing out as important.
>
> Marketing staff became increasingly alarmed and expressed their concerns regarding this overly cluttered home page to the CEO, who in turn expressed concerns to the board. Such concerns fell on deaf ears. There was historical precedent for active board involvement in staff operations and the

CEO, lacking confidence and having concerns about her job security, refused to make the issue a hill to die on.

Over time the association suffered a substantial drop in the number of website visitors. There were fewer drill-downs and less time spent on the website. The marketing department's plans and budgets for promoting specific high priority, timely events and products had to be significantly revised because staff could no longer count on the website to generate sufficient interest and revenue. More time and expense had to be directed to alternative marketing vehicles, both hard copy and email traffic, than otherwise would have been the case.

Meanwhile, the association's members became increasingly frustrated and dissatisfied in their ability to navigate the website and locate items of interest to them. This was evidenced by the number of complaints directed to staff and the results of member surveys. Marketing staff were increasingly demoralized, leading to unwanted turnover and difficulty in recruiting replacements.

Exacerbating the situation were perceptions on the part of members and staff alike that the association's primary competitor had a well-organized website that served as a true marketing tool. It was clear from data analytics that, in contrast to association M, the competitor website was experiencing significant growth in its website traffic.

Ultimately there was a successful grassroots push among association M's members to overhaul its website, but significant damage had already been done. It took years before the organization recovered.

This case study aptly illustrates how a series of individual marketing decisions can have a snowball effect. When 10, 20, or more member leaders view themselves as marketing experts, their collective input and demands can be devastating to the association's brand and overall strategic marketing of products, programs, and services.

This is not just a case of having too many cooks in the kitchen. Marketing is a profession! Similar to any profession, there is accumulated knowledge, dos, don'ts, and best practices that are acquired by formal education and years of experience.

Board members and other association leaders should certainly convey opinions about marketing to staff professionals. Best marketing practices call for the professionals to actively elicit opinions through surveys, focus groups, and other member research vehicles. But final marketing decisions should rest primarily with staff. The board should hold staff accountable for results relative to member satisfaction, member awareness of what the association offers, and revenue generation from these offerings.

Exhibit 2.4 provides a more detailed articulation of how selected marketing roles might be handled in an association where member leaders are appropriately focused on governance and the staff on operations. Note that references in the matrix to CEO decision making infers significant delegation to the marketing department head.

Exhibit 2.4

Marketing Management Role Definition

Role Key

D = Decision maker, I = Involved, and N = Notified

Role	Officers	Board	Board Committee (if applicable)	CEO/Staff	Clarifying Details
Determine member research techniques and protocols		N	I?	D	Member research data, typically acquired through survey processes, are crucial to assist the board and staff in decision making. However, care needs to be taken not to over-survey members and thereby create survey fatigue. Although maybe not subject matter experts, perhaps a board committee can provide guidance on survey topics, questions to ask, and identify potential participants, and the staff makes final decisions in this regard.
Set prices for products, programs, and services		I		D	The board determines expected revenue generation and profitability for the association's overall portfolio of offerings through the budgeting process. The CEO manages to these overall expectations, using defined methodologies to establish price points for individual offerings. Note: The board may elect to retain selected pricing decisions (e.g., annual meeting registration fees).

Role	Officers	Board	Board Committee (if applicable)	CEO/Staff	Clarifying Details
Finalize marketing plans		I		D	The board, keeping in mind the strategic plan, sets overall expectations for marketing plan results, including member awareness targets and revenue generation. The CEO oversees development of product/program/service-specific marketing plans (e.g., channels, frequency and type of messaging, and budgets) to achieve the desired outcomes. The board is notified of plan highlights during the course of their review and approval of the budget.
Finalize marketing collateral		N	I	D	The CEO has overall responsibility for all collateral material development, ensuring appropriate imagery and messaging to be effective and provide expected ROI. Subject matter experts, perhaps a board committee, will be engaged to help ensure messaging is correct and appropriate to the target audience.
Design the website		I	I	D	Staff has overall responsibility for website design, including the overall structure of web pages and navigation. Member input regarding design decisions is critical and will be sought on many levels, including the board, perhaps a board committee, and members representing various demographic groups.
Determine content for the website and social media		N	I	D	Subject matter experts, perhaps including a board committee as well as other member leaders, contribute to and influence the content of website and social media marketing pieces. The ultimate content decisions are made under the CEO's authority.

• • •

Public and Media Relations Management

Public and media relations cross all boundaries and can affect an association in many ways. Unfortunately, many board members often view it as a simple activity. They believe all it involves is calling a reporter and "getting them to write a story" about a member or the association. It does not work that way! Board members are often so engaged in their association that they assume everything that they do is important or, in other words, is news. But reporters do not care unless they think their readers will care.

What reporters think is news is also often the last thing that an association wants to talk about in public, and this is particularly true in a crisis communications situation. Note the following case study:

> Association G had a major failure in one of its core businesses, resulting in national negative press in both the trade and mainstream media. This association did not have a sound crisis communication plan in place, and decision makers were slow to react. The board chair, who by policy was the official media spokesperson, was hesitant to do anything. Several other board members and the association's attorney advocated a bunker approach—the opposite of crisis communications best practice. This hesitancy was bolstered by the CEO, who did not want to overstep his bounds with the board.
>
> The entire staff communication team, from the media contact person to the VP of communication, advocated a more open, proactive approach that would focus on changing the tone of the stories being written from one of failure to one of solution finding. This advice was ignored.
>
> As the days moved on, what began as a single crusade by one investigative reporter turned into a media feeding frenzy, in large part because of the lack of public response from the association. The communication department was hamstrung because of the risk-adverse, hesitant board, its chair, and the CEO. Eventually the issue bled over from the media to regulators and legislators. This resulted in Congressional hearings and another round of negative publicity for the association and its members.
>
> These problems were a direct result of the association's leadership ignoring input from its professional staff and over-relying on legal opinions, with little or no initial concern for public opinion.

Crisis communication situations like this one can rarely be predicted. However, for many associations it is only a matter of time before one will pop up. Aside from associations representing communication industry professionals, it's unlikely many other associations will have board officers or other member leaders who have the requisite expertise and experience to lead the charge in responding to negative publicity.

Associations should not rely on the board chair, as happened in the above example, to make key communication/public relations decisions. They should instead rely on the expertise of communication professionals on staff or a previously retained public relations firm to lead the charge. Doing so will not necessarily make negative publicity go away, but the impact can be minimized. In some instances, publicity that is initially negative for the association can be turned around to positive if the association is viewed as concerned and proactive in addressing a problem.

Exhibit 2.5 provides a more detailed articulation of how selected public and media relations roles might be handled in an association where member leaders are appropriately focused on governance and the staff on operations. Note that references in the matrix to CEO decision making infers significant delegation to the public relations department head.

Exhibit 2.5

Public and Media Management Role Definition

Role Key

D = Decision maker, I = Involved, and N = Notified

Role	Officers	Board	Board Committee (if applicable)	CEO/Staff	Clarifying Details
Develop a public and media relations plan		N		D	Staff develops the plan annually, including a proposed budget.
Throughout the year, determine what needs to be communicated to which external audiences		N		D	The staff leader assigned with public and media management accountability (i.e., CEO or director of communication), determines which press releases will be generated and which interview requests from various media sources will be granted.
Generate content of communications to the media	I	N		D	Staff generates the specific content of press releases as well as talking points that will be conveyed to designated media spokespeople. Depending on the sensitivity of the situation, staff may consult with the chair or his/her designee regarding what is conveyed. Quotes attributed to specific member leaders are approved by the member leaders before dissemination.

Role	Officers	Board	Board Committee (if applicable)	CEO/Staff	Clarifying Details
Engage and manage external PR firm relationship(s)		N		D	Staff, ideally based on an RFP process and subject to budgetary constraints, selects appropriate external PR resources to meet the association's needs for continuing public and media relationship management.
Select media spokespeople	D			I	The chair or his/her designee determines, in consultation with staff, who will be designated spokespeople depending upon the situation involved. Staff provides training to the selected individuals.
Develop and maintain a crisis communication plan		D		I	Staff develops the initial crisis communication plan for board approval and assures that it is continually kept up-to-date.
Respond to PR crisis events	I	N		D	Accountability for crisis plan execution resides with the professionals (i.e., the CEO or her/his designee) in consultation with the chair and perhaps other officers.

• • •

Similar to the guidance provided above, associations will be well served if their leaders give attention to every key functional area. They should identify typical decisions that must be made on a recurring basis, clearly assign decision-making accountability, and make sure these assignments are made to the individuals and entities best positioned by expertise, experience, and time to make them.

And the Buck Stops With...

The board officers, other member leaders, and staff leaders collectively should collaborate in creating and maintaining the right mindset of assigning roles and decision-making accountability where it is best suited to benefit the organization and its members. This will by no means be easy because it involves taking and keeping power away from individuals and entities that are used to being in the driver's seat and may have selfish reasons for maintaining the status quo.

The chair and the CEO, by virtue of their stature in the organization, need to work closely and take the lead roles in building a platform for change. They should convey how current role assignments have resulted in bad decision making that has jeopardized the organization's ability to compete in the marketplace and add value for its members. Governance consultants can help by sharing case studies from other organizations that illustrate both problems resulting from poor role assignments and success stories resulting from appropriately assigned roles.

The CEO is best positioned to drive the initial development of decision-making matrices. He/she should also assure such documents are reviewed and updated by the board and staff at least biannually.

The individual or entity charged with board and other member leader orientations should ensure that the matrices are thoroughly understood by new member leaders, and the CEO is similarly responsible for ensuring they are understood by the staff

Finally, the chair must serve as the primary enforcer because 99 percent of the challenges to assigned decision-making authority will come from fellow board members and other member leaders. The CEO needs to be a strong coach and supporter of the chair in undertaking this role.

Tying It Back to the Members

Often an individual rises through an organization, not just associations, and reaches a point where he/she views the organization as "my sandbox," making decisions that others are much better positioned to make. The results can be harmful, even disastrous, for the organization's current and future success, as in the site selection for an annual meeting mentioned earlier in this chapter.

When decision making resides with the right individuals and entities, an organization is well positioned to flourish. Decisions will be more thought through and based on previously accumulated knowledge. They will be made by those who have the relevant education, expertise, and experience to assess alternatives and select the right one to implement. It will be far less likely that decisions are made based on whims or mere opinions of powerful members or staff leaders.

Good decisions will tie directly to increasing member value and maintaining an organizational structure that is efficient and cost effective. This will give the association a leg up on meeting its competitive and operational challenges.

SECTION 2

Performing Your Key Fiduciary Duties Well

CHAPTER 3

Understand Your Basic Fiduciary Duties

BOARD MEMBERS IN EVERY ORGANIZATION, including the CEO if not formally serving on the board, are charged with fulfilling a set of fiduciary duties. These should be addressed in board orientation and reinforced as needed by in-house or external legal counsel. Many of these duties extend to committee members and other leaders within the governance structure.

The first duty is **care.** Directors should demonstrate competence in performing directorial functions and act as a reasonably prudent person would in a like position and under similar circumstances. The duty of care includes:

- Acting in good faith;
- Reading agenda materials and in other ways being prepared for meetings;
- Participating in meetings, including asking questions to clarify understanding; and
- Exercising independent judgment, as opposed to blindly following the lead of a board colleague(s).

A second core duty is **loyalty.** Loyalty requires that directors faithfully pursue the interests of the organization. The association's interests should be prioritized above all interests a given director has relative to her/his personal well-being, the interests of another person, or the interests of another organization. Directors may not use their service on the board, including information that is made available to them, to secure personal benefit. They should disclose actual, potential, or perceived conflicts of interest. As a result, they may be required to abstain from participating in certain board discussions and decisions. This duty also calls for directors to maintain confidentiality of all board discussions.

Finally, there is the duty of **obedience**. Directors should faithfully pursue the organization's mission and decisions within the bounds of the law. They must adhere to the organization's policies and procedures. And even if they disagree, they should support and help implement decisions made by the board as a whole.

With these core duties in mind, boards have a number of specific fiduciary roles. The following chapters address roles that are most critical to the success of associations and to support the best interests of their members. Although some association boards are stellar performers, most boards and their leaders struggle with one or more of these roles. While acknowledging the challenges, fiduciary roles can be successfully undertaken if association leaders adopt the right mindset and carefully consider and implement suggestions, techniques, and tools used by high-performing boards.

A final note regarding the next chapter in this section, which addresses a situation you may not be currently facing—the need to select a new CEO. Although it may be tempting to skip this chapter, it is important to realize that most CEO vacancies occur suddenly and unexpectedly. Having an understanding of how best to handle such a transition well in advance of it occurring can mitigate what can be a very stressful time for the board and organization.

CHAPTER 4

Select and Onboard Your CEO Wisely

PERHAPS THE BIGGEST FIDUCIARY CHALLENGE, as well as opportunity, that a board faces is its relationship with the CEO. There is no limit to what an association can accomplish when:

- An association has the right CEO in place;
- The CEO and board are in sync with their respective roles and responsibilities; and
- There is an atmosphere of mutual trust and support.

Conversely, the wrong CEO, or a dysfunctional board/CEO working relationship can suck the life out of an organization. Dealing with the relationship itself becomes the primary focus of the board's attention. The negativity permeates far beyond the board room—recognized by the headquarters staff and among rank and file association members.

Taken to an extreme, the relationship all too often in the association world results in CEO turnover, which can be extremely costly in legal fees and severance compensation. Even if the CEO departs voluntarily, there are significant out-of-pocket expenses in finding a replacement. This can amount to one third or more of a new CEO's first-year compensation when a search firm is employed to assist in hiring a replacement.

In addition, there are expenses associated with search committee members' and candidate travel and hidden expenses resulting from taking these individuals away from their day jobs. And do not forget to consider relocation and other expenses to bring the next CEO on board. The total out-of-pocket CEO turnover expense can easily extend into six figures and for some situations over a million dollars. Not the best use of membership dues!

More critical than lost money is lost momentum. The search process can easily take six months to a year or more before the new CEO is in place and sufficiently oriented to the point of making a difference. Key staff members, especially those loyal to the previous CEO, worry about their own futures, dust off their resumes, and spend less time and energy on their jobs. Boards typically are reluctant to undertake anything new or make significant changes until the new CEO is in place. Meanwhile, the competition moves forward to catch up or surpass the value provided to the association's current and potential members.

All organizations periodically experience situations where the changing operating environment calls for new staff leadership. However, associations face two key, unique challenges that tend to increase the likelihood of dysfunctional board/CEO working relationships. These challenges all too often lead to termination of a CEO who in other regards is performing admirably on behalf of the association.

The first challenge is the annual change in board leadership that is typical for most associations. It would be one thing if each new board chair had the same competencies, strengths, weaknesses, leadership style, and personality. Obviously this is never the case. Just when the CEO and his primary supervisor, the board chair, have hit their stride with their working relationship, it is time for that chair to move on and a new one to take the helm.

The CEO faces additional challenges relative to annual turnover of the supervisory relationship if there is dysfunctionality, including political turmoil, within the board itself. In one association I worked with there was a period of four years during which the board chairs came from the same political faction of the board. In spite of the CEO's attempts to act and be perceived as neutral, after the four-year period, she was identified by the out-of-power faction as the "enemy." When the board chair position switched for a two-year period to the faction previously out of power, the new chair's working relationship with the CEO was doomed from the start. By the end of the two-year period, the CEO had left the organization in spite of otherwise stellar organizational and personal performance during her tenure.

The second challenge, usually not found in the corporate world, relates to the composition of boards and other governance entities. In my experience, many association boards, most notably professional societies, are populated by individuals who have not previously had significant experience leading or serving on the boards of multi-million dollar entities. Their previous experience interacting with CEOs is at times limited, unless directly reporting to a CEO in their day jobs. Now thrust into the role of a board member or officer, they may find themselves interacting with a CEO on a different level. It is not easy for many of them to make that transition, and it puts extra pressure on everyone to make the relationship work.

For the Good of the Members

Some associations navigate the afore-mentioned challenges well. They have long-tenured CEOs who enjoy productive working relationships with their boards and each new set of board officers. These CEOs, secure in their relationship with the board, can devote more energy to advancing the interests of the association and its members.

When there inevitably is CEO turnover in these associations, their leaders carefully execute the CEO succession plan (more about succession plans in Chapter 8) and take the appropriate steps to secure new staff leadership. What are the secrets for success in selecting a new CEO? Following are some best practices associations, and more specifically their search committees, should take. This advice is accumulated from search firm professionals who focus much of their work on the association community.

- Jill Christie, President, Tuft & Associates, Chicago, Illinois
- Lorraine Lavet, National Practice Leader and Senior Client Partner, Korn/Ferry International, Reston, Virginia
- Wendy Pangburn, Managing Director, Pangburn Partners, Washington, DC
- Leonard Pfeiffer, Managing Director, Pfeiffer & Company, Washington, DC
- Robert Van Hook, Principal & Chief Transition Evangelist, Transition Management Consulting, San Diego, California
- Jim Zaniello, President, Vetted Solutions, Washington, DC

Make the Right Staff Leadership Decision During the Transition Period

Regardless of why your CEO leaves the association, a decision needs to be made quickly regarding who will keep the ship running until the next CEO is selected. Many associations rely on a team of current staff leaders, a board member, or another association member for this critical role. Although these options may involve the least upfront out-of-pocket expense, they could prove costly in other ways. Such individuals, given their other commitments, may not have sufficient time to handle the full-time role of a

CEO, especially if the association is facing a highly competitive or turbulent operating environment.

Two alternatives for transitional staff leadership are worth considering—testing an heir apparent or hiring an interim CEO. If there is an heir apparent in the staff, the departure of the CEO presents a good opportunity to test that individual for the CEO role, provided much of that individual's previous accountabilities can be transferred to other staff or contractors.

Even if there is such an individual, Robert Van Hook says many associations find that engaging a professional interim CEO is the best choice for the organization (see sidebar). A professional interim CEO can help ensure the organization maintains its forward momentum during this critical time, provide a fresh perspective relative to association operations, and in some cases serve as a "healer" to the staff. Professional interim CEOs are experienced in entering organizations during transition periods and are not encumbered with a need to posture for the permanent CEO role. They have a job to do, they do it in a relatively short time, and they move on to a new role with another organization.

Take Care Selecting Search Committee Members

Many times an association will populate the search committee with past presidents and other long-tenured, well-recognized leaders to vet and select the next CEO. Although it is certainly helpful to include a few individuals with historical perspective, the majority of committee members should include current and future association leaders. After all, these are the individuals most attuned to the association's future needs and the leaders with whom the new CEO will be working closely with in future years to strategize and implement new courses of action.

Hire a Search Firm to Select Your Next CEO

If there is a logical, consensus heir-apparent to the previous CEO within the staff organization, an individual who has a clear ability to lead the association into the future, then by all means hire her or him. However, without such a consensus, it is best to engage outside assistance in selecting your next CEO because of the expertise, experience, and resources they can provide to:

- Create a profile of the ideal CEO for the organization;
- Advertise and in other ways recruit candidates to apply for the position;
- Vet the sometimes hundreds of possible candidates who express interest; and
- Ultimately narrow down the field to the best candidate.

Ready, Fire, Aim?

By Robert Van Hook, Principal and Chief Transition Evangelist, Transition Management Consulting, San Diego, California

When a CEO vacancy occurs, boards of directors justifiably feel a need to fill the vacancy immediately. The CEO's departure creates a power vacuum and a level of uncertainty that often pushes the board to move to executive search before it is clear about the organization's future direction. Before beginning the search, the board should strive for consensus about where the organization is going, what worked and didn't work with the last executive, and what kinds of executive skills and characteristics the next CEO will need to be successful.

An executive search is a two-way activity—the board is looking for a CEO who fits with the association's needs and culture, and CEO candidates are looking for a great place to engage their skills and be successful. The organization may not be ready to hire a successor CEO when:

- The departing CEO has had a long tenure with the organization;
- The departing CEO has "retired-in-place;"
- The CEO's departure was abrupt or messy;
- There is turmoil within the staff and/or volunteers;
- The organization has significant operational problems and the board wants the successor CEO to deal with strategy rather than administrative fixes.

In these situations and others, the board may wish to consider engaging an external professional interim CEO. An interim CEO can give the board time to "aim" before it "fires"—to get the organization ready for a successor CEO. Engaging a professional interim CEO gives the board time to deal with transitional issues and, when the time is right, conduct its search for a new staff leader in a thoughtful mode with the assurance that the organization is well-managed during the transition period.

An external interim CEO:

- Provides experienced, professional executive management of staff and operations during the transition;
- Maintains critical internal and external relationships with members, customers, affiliates, sponsors, vendors, grantors, and related organizations;
- Supports the board and staff in dealing with the human aspects of change during the executive transition period;
- Assesses operations and systems and recommends improvements to the board;
- Helps the board prepare for a successful executive search; and
- Works with the board to effect a smooth, seamless transition to a successor executive, which could involve either mentoring a current staff leader into the CEO role or integrating a new leader from outside the organization.

Perhaps most important in many transition situations, the interim CEO can execute change that is difficult for a permanent CEO to make. This includes, in some instances, eliminating politically powerful staff whom the previous CEO may have lacked the courage to terminate and whom a new CEO might perceive as unpleasant albatrosses with whom to deal.

An incoming CEO has a limited number of goodwill credits, and it is important for the interim CEO to take credit-draining organizational changes off the successor executive's plate. Otherwise, the new CEO could spend a lion's share of goodwill credits dealing with a personnel issue that could and should have been dealt with before the new CEO's arrival. The new CEO should be able to come in with a focus on building positive partnerships with the board and advancing the organization's strategy.

The transition between CEOs is a time ripe with possibilities for creativity and change. During these periods, organizations can improve operations and often enhance, not just maintain, organizational momentum. A good interim CEO skillfully assesses operations and relationships and then resolves the issues for the next CEO. A professional interim CEO works with the staff and board to create a positive climate of expectation and readiness for the successor.

Even very large, sophisticated associations with search committees composed of high-caliber executives or professionals possessing demonstrated competence in making CEO hiring decisions frequently need external assistance in sourcing and assessing candidates.

In the case of internal candidates, a good search firm can handle the politics, providing an informed, unbiased third-party perspective that can compare such individuals with external candidates.

Hire the Best Firm for Your Needs

According to Lorraine Lavet, the specific needs of an association will dictate whether a large, well-known firm or a small boutique one is best suited to your needs. For example, some associations' primary need may be identifying unique, out-of-the-box candidates, ones that may come to light only via the wide-reaching tentacles of a very large executive search firm. Other associations may be content with looking at a narrower set of candidates (e.g., primarily current association executives) but require more hand-holding in undertaking specific steps traditionally associated with a search process. This circumstance may be compatible with what a small boutique firm can offer at a more competitive price.

Fortunately, there are a number of executive search firms with different sizes, methodologies, experience, and competencies to consider. *CEO Update,* a periodical highlighting CEO job opportunities in associations and other nonprofit organizations, is a great resource for an association's search committee to use in identifying appropriate executive search firms for consideration. Each monthly issue lists active searches facilitated by various firms, giving a feel for the type of clientele they serve.

In selecting your search firm, be careful not to rely too much on price comparisons; the adage "you get what you pay for" sometimes applies. Leonard Pfeiffer notes an example of a long-time client who, in an effort to save fees, selected another search firm for a complicated, difficult executive search assignment because the fees were significantly below what Pfeiffer quoted. The executive who was ultimately selected lasted only eight months. The resulting turmoil during and after his tenure constituted a significant setback for the organization. Months later Leonard learned from one of the association's members that the other search firm didn't do background and reference checks of the candidate before recommending him. As the member put it, "Had they done so, they would have quickly learned the guy was all show and no go."

Heed Advice From Search Professionals

An experienced search firm professional will develop a solid understanding of the association's operating environment as well as needs and desires the board has for its next staff leader. This understanding drives every subsequent step of the search process, including the identification of a short list of candidates for consideration by the search committee. Following are key words of wisdom from the aforementioned panel of search firm professionals.

Devote Sufficient Time to The Process

It is natural for the board and search committee to want to move quickly through the search process. They often forget the complexities and logistical challenges associated with:

- Scheduling search firm interviews with prospective candidates;
- Comparing potentially hundreds of candidates to develop the short list; and
- Working around the busy schedules of search committee members and candidates to arrive at dates that work for what are typically two rounds of final candidate interviews.

At best, a good CEO search will take three to four months to complete. More typically, the search process extends from six months to a year and sometimes longer.

Start With the Profile

Understandably, many search committee members are anxious to immediately identify candidates whom they perceive should be on the short list of new CEO candidates. In many cases they push for individuals who are similar to the departing CEO or, if the relationship with that individual was strained, individuals who are completely different. As tempting as it may be to move quickly, it is critical for the association to take a long, hard look at the organization, the environment it anticipates operating in over the next three to five years or more, and the type of staff leader who is best positioned to serve the organization well during that timeframe. Search firm professionals should be given latitude and time to create the profile of experience, competencies, skills, and attributes that will serve as the primary basis for identifying and attracting the best possible candidates for the position.

Achieve Consensus With the Profile

A profile is helpful only if it is truly supported by all search committee members. Wendy Pangburn relates a situation she faced when a profile was developed and approved by the search committee, but apparently several members merely gave it lip service, maintaining their own ideas of the ideal profile for their new CEO. Consequently, the search process broke down when candidates were presented to the search committee for final consideration. Committee members who deep down did not agree with the original profile now registered strong objections to candidates who matched the profile, but did not fit their personal agendas. As a result, the candidate pool was scrapped and the search process essentially began again from scratch. Lesson learned? When crafting the candidate profile, it is critical to have candid, even if uncomfortable, discussions to attain true consensus. Doing so will make the rest of the search process flow much smoother and will more likely result in an appropriate selection.

Avoid Limiting the Candidate Pool

Jim Zaniello advises association search committees to think broadly about the future to ensure they seek the right qualities in their next executive. Some association search committees, in some instances constrained by the organizational bylaws, take a narrow posture, such as requiring that a CEO comes from the membership base, without considering what the association truly needs. For example, a nursing society may require a nurse CEO, or a trade association representing electronics manufacturing companies may require an engineer CEO.

A from-the-membership requirement is totally appropriate when there is an expectation that the CEO serves as the primary spokesperson of the association to external stakeholders, such as representing the organization at Congressional hearings or responding to most or all media requests to interview a representative from the organization. Such situations require the spokesperson to have detailed knowledge, expertise, and experience pertaining to the specific profession or trade, along with the credibility that goes with it.

However, many association boards prefer to have the board chair or other member leaders serve in the spokesperson capacity, with the CEO relegated to a coaching capacity. Such a posture may or may not be the best approach for a given association. There are plenty of examples where the member leader spokesperson model has worked well, and likewise examples where such leaders have been woefully inadequate in representing the association.

Regardless of right or wrong, when members are the association's primary spokespeople, maintaining a from-the-membership-base requirement for selecting a CEO unnecessarily limits the pool of candidates. It may result in the association's losing out on one or more tremendous association leader candidates who could be best suited to guide the organization to future success, and thereby best serve the members.

Such individuals may have had no previous exposure to the association's profession or trade. But they have a track record of quickly getting up to speed on the operating environments, challenges, and opportunities an association's members face. They understand how associations work and have the ability to marshal resources, member leaders, and staff to better serve members, grow the organization, and improve its operations. They rely on and coach the appropriate member leaders to serve effectively as spokespeople in the relatively infrequent situations when that role is required. Unlike a CEO candidate from the membership base who may have vested interest in a specific demographic or subspecialty constituency, an outsider typically carries no biases.

If there are to be any limitations placed on the new CEO candidate pool, rather than having a from-the-membership-base requirement, it may be more relevant and appropriate to require a strong association profession background. It is easy to lose sight of the fact that association leadership is a profession itself, including its own certification—Certified Association Executive (CAE). Association CEOs and other staff leaders operate in work environments with which most association members are unfamiliar. Association governance structures and composition are frequently complex and challenging to navigate. The interactions associations have with their customers—primarily members—are different from the corporate world because these customers in many instances have an ownership or entitlement mentality. The portfolio of a typical association's products, programs, and services is far more diverse than other entities, ranging from educational products and courses to meetings, publications, practice guidelines, standards, advocacy, affinity programs, and more. There are also unique requirements for building relationships with corporate and advocacy partners.

Bottom line, it is frequently easier for an incoming CEO with strong association management credentials to quickly gain an understanding of the association's profession or trade than it is for a from-the-membership CEO to learn how to lead an association.

Strategize Compensation to Attract the Best Candidates

A vacant CEO position can easily attract a large pool of candidates. However, the number of candidates is not important. Rather it is the caliber of those applying that determines whether the board will have a choice of solid finalists or will find itself scrambling to find even one who minimally fits the bill.

A board may have limited control over the factors playing into candidates' decisions to apply or not apply for the CEO position (e.g., size of the budget and staff, perceived opportunities for professional growth, or current location of the headquarters office). However, the board can affect the candidate pool in how it answers two strategic compensation-related questions:

1. How should the competitive market be defined in assessing the CEO's compensation package?

The market is typically defined relative to industry, size, and geography. These definitions should be based on the type of organization from which the association is likely to recruit its next CEO. Following are example industry definitions:

- A subset of associations (e.g., all engineering societies);
- All associations; and
- A mixture of associations and companies composing the membership base (e.g., electronics companies for the corresponding trade association).

In terms of size, many compensation consultants recommend the market be defined as organizations with operating budgets that are half to double the size of your organization. Finally, the geography should typically correspond with the geographic reach of your association—national for a national association or state for a state association.

So, putting it all together, the market definition for a specific association, assuming the association's budget is $5 million, could be stated as "all internationally focused associations primarily composed of physician members and having operating budgets between $2.5 and $10 million."

2. How should the CEO's overall compensation be positioned relative to the defined competitive market—below, at, or above the median?

The answer to this question will go a long way toward determining the caliber of candidates your association will attract in filling a vacant CEO position. An organization may get away with below market compensation if the board is satisfied with candidates who have no previous CEO experience. The position may also attract previous CEOs who, to use a sports analogy, are solid back-ups or second-string players. But the best and brightest CEO candidates will typically stay away and choose to pursue other opportunities.

After the CEO is hired, maintaining a below market strategy is risky if the board hopes to retain a high performing CEO for more than a few years. CEOs are typically well-aware of their value and will be vulnerable to alternative CEO opportunities that are presented to them.

Some boards ignore these questions and rely on the compensation package of the recently-departed CEO as a guide for compensating the next CEO. Doing so can be a mistake. If the previous CEO left voluntarily, an inadequate compensation package may have played into her/his decision to leave. Even if the previous CEO did not leave voluntarily, the compensation market for CEO positions can change rather significantly even in two to three years. Therefore, the board should listen carefully to advice offered by its search firm professionals regarding what to offer candidates. Zaniello recommends association board leaders engage an outside expert to conduct a CEO compensation and benefits analysis. Such analyses are valuable not only as part of the search process, but also periodically thereafter (i.e., every two or three years) to ensure the CEO is compensated appropriately and not at risk to leave because of uncompetitive compensation levels.

Ask the Right Questions

Search committees should strongly consider advice from search firm professionals in constructing the list of questions asked of final candidates for the CEO position. Having gone through the search process scores if not hundreds of times, search professionals have seen first-hand great questions to separate the wheat from the chaff, helping to drive selection of the best candidate for the job. They are also keenly aware of the types of questions that cannot or should not be asked, including ones that could place the association in legal jeopardy.

Be Transparent With Information

Jill Christie recommends association leaders be honest and transparent with information. This means sharing relevant documents (e.g., financial statements) with candidates to ensure they are aware of key strategic, financial, legal, or other issues they will be faced with if awarded the position. Their reactions during the interview process to this information may be critical in assessing fit with the association. It will also help prepare the selected candidate to hit the ground running when he/she is hired.

Maintain Confidentiality

Pangburn has witnessed the impact of search committee members who ignored her pleas for confidentiality, ensuring all conversations about candidates stay strictly within the bounds of committee deliberations. In one case, a committee member conveyed the names of final candidates who were not selected to an individual in a social setting. That individual had ties to a board member from the organization where one of the candidates served as the CEO. Word got out that the CEO was in the job market, which ultimately was used as an excuse to terminate him.

In an example provided by Pfeiffer, a top candidate for the CEO position didn't lose his current job but withdrew his candidacy at the last minute of the search process. Apparently the candidate's current boss learned, as a result of casual conversation with a search committee member, that he was about to lose his key employee. The candidate indicated he had been confronted by the managing partner and asked to confirm his intention to stay or to leave. He opted to save his current job rather than take a chance he ultimately wouldn't be selected as the association's new CEO.

Search committee members should never, during or after the search process is complete, divulge the names of candidates who were considered but not selected. Nor should they discuss with others outside the committee specifics of the vetting process or votes taken in narrowing down the field and ultimately making the final selection.

Overall, treat your selected search firm professionals as the partners they want to be with you. Your success is their success in picking the right person for the job.

Commit to Comprehensive CEO Onboarding

Once the selection of a new CEO has been made, it is crucial to get the individual off to a good start. The first three to six months can make or break the CEO and her/his relationship with the board. A key to success involves giving careful consideration to the onboarding process. The CEO needs a clear understanding of the operating environment he/she is walking into, the expected roles and decision-making parameters associated with the board and CEO, anticipated communication protocols, and performance expectations.

Unfortunately, many association boards and new CEOs give little attention to the onboarding process. The Bridgespan Group recently conducted a study that addressed onboarding, with results appearing in the *Stanford Social Innovation Review.* The study results pointed to the lack of a hands-on role boards take when onboarding new nonprofit CEOs, which is preparing them for their new roles and helping them settle into the job. A few data points from the study:

- Only 39 percent of respondents disagreed with the statement, "My board was effective in helping me set priorities the first year."

- Some 50 percent of CEOs did not clarify with their boards how they would work together in the first few months on the job.
- Some 66 percent of CEOs disagreed with the statement, "The board and I worked effectively together to establish concrete measures and milestones for the board to use to assess my performance in my first year."

Following are specific components of an effective new CEO onboarding program.

Perform Key Stakeholder Assessments

Any incoming CEO would find it helpful to have the pulse of the current operating environment from the perspective of key stakeholder groups. The first key stakeholder group is the board itself. The interim period between the previous and new CEO is an ideal time to administer a board self-assessment survey, using either the BoardSource and ASAE tool mentioned in Chapter 1 or an equivalent. The results will point to strengths as well as developmental needs the new CEO should be attuned to from the start of her/his tenure.

A second level of assessment is member perceptions. If your association does not have a strong pulse of members' needs, expectations, and opinions of your association, the interim period between the previous and new CEO is a great time to obtain it, ideally through a combination of surveys, focus groups, and other approaches suggested by marketing and membership professionals on your staff.

Speaking of staff, the incoming CEO may have been told about the overall state of staff morale and the strengths and weaknesses of key staff leaders. But are these perceptions accurate? Not necessarily. The interim period presents a great opportunity to perform a staff satisfaction and engagement survey. Such a survey, assuming staff are candid, can be helpful to the new CEO in identifying core areas of strength to build on as well as concerns that need to be addressed in the near term. It also can be useful as a baseline for subsequently achieving improvement in staff perceptions, assuming the instrument is re-administered a year or two into the new CEO's tenure.

A second level of staff assessment pertains to individual staff leaders. At a minimum, before coming onboard, the new CEO should be given access to the most recent performance assessments of each of these individuals.

The interim period may also be an ideal time to administer a 360-degree feedback process of staff leaders using one of many tools in the marketplace to anonymously gather input from each direct report's peers, subordinates, and perhaps the board itself regarding strengths and development opportunities. Having access to the resulting assessments can be valuable to the incoming CEO in establishing working relationships with all direct reports and managing their performance.

On the flip side, if the organization does not have a history of using 360s, the process may be perceived as overly disruptive and threatening to staff, leading to decreased morale and perhaps unwanted turnover. If such surveys are not undertaken, as a partial substitute, the board chair or officer group should be prepared to share with the new CEO their perceptions of each of the CEO's direct reports based on their personal experiences as well as what they have heard anecdotally from other member leaders and staff.

A final level of assessment that can be helpful to incoming CEOs consists of the perceptions of key external stakeholders, including corporate supporters, advocacy partners, and entities teaming with the association on education content development. Do they view your association favorably or are there significant concerns that need to be addressed? These and related questions can be asked in-person, by telephone, or as part of a survey.

Typically the best approach to undertaking the numerous types of assessments just mentioned during the interim between the previous and new CEO is reliance on an independent, external resource(s). Alternatives include the executive search firm, a consulting firm, or the interim CEO, especially if the interim has a consulting background and has interacted with and served numerous similar entities. He/she can leverage such experiences in reviewing assessment results and identifying improvement opportunities for the new CEO's consideration.

Implement a Good Communication Plan

A marketing or communication staff member or an outside firm should develop a comprehensive communication plan after the CEO has been selected. Craft announcements to the media, members in leadership positions, general members, and staff that convey a positive welcome and highlight the new CEO's qualifications.

The communication plan should extend beyond written announcements. Association board members should take the initiative to introduce the new CEO to their key contacts, influential insiders, key sponsors, vendors, regulators, and leaders of affiliated organizations.

Establish a Transition Team

Christie suggests a small transition team of three or four individuals be appointed by the board to work with the new CEO during the first six months of her or his tenure. Transition team members serve as advisors, coaches, and a sounding board for the new executive. These advisors could include, at a minimum, the search committee chair, president-elect, and treasurer. The new CEO should schedule a weekly conference call with the transition team during the first three months and then monthly for the next three months, seeking advice and input on transition issues. The new CEO often faces legacy relationships, historical landmines, and sometimes difficult staff leadership dynamics that require, and can benefit from, the private and confidential advice of a trusted transition team.

For example, Christie describes how a new CEO benefited from the support of her transition team. "When the new CEO replaced a long-term, beloved executive, several unexpected landmines surfaced. The biggest problem was an internal candidate who did not get the job and who seemed intent on sabotaging the new executive. The CEO discussed the situation with her transition team, which provided historical perspective on the individual plus helpful advice and guidance. Most important, the team was available to listen. Ultimately, the CEO established a positive working relationship with the internal candidate, resulting in a win-win for the CEO, staff, and leadership."

Clarify Board/CEO Roles and Communication Protocols

Having gone through a number of association CEO search processes as a candidate, I can personally attest to how little attention is given to role definition and communication protocols before an offer is made and the candidate accepts the position. Search firm professionals, given limitations of search committee time and attention, discourage candidates from getting too much into the weeds when asking such questions.

Unless a concerted effort is made by the board chair or new CEO to address these topics before or shortly after the new CEO is onboard, everyone can easily fly blindly in the weeks, months, and even years that follow. In the process, differing expectations can result in unintentional and unnecessary friction in relationships that the CEO is cultivating with the board chair, board members, and other key member leaders.

That is why it is so important to address the type of specific role definition topics presented in Chapter 2. If a decision-making matrix is not already documented and agreed on, one should be established within the first three months of the new CEO's tenure.

Clarity also is needed relative to the CEO's role in specific situations. For example, during board meetings is there an expectation that the CEO be treated similarly to any other board member, other than voting, with freedom and encouragement to actively contribute to all discussions? Hopefully so! Or is there instead an expectation that the CEO's role is primarily to provide secretarial support to the chair during board meetings, speaking only when called upon?

Similarly, what is the CEO's expected role when accompanying the chair or other member leaders to meetings involving key stakeholders, including corporate sponsors, vendors, and advocacy coalition partners? Should the CEO take the lead in representing the association and interacting with representatives from these organizations, or is there an expectation that he/she be viewed as a supporting player?

All communication protocols should be defined in terms of expected CEO interactions with the chair, other board officers, the executive committee as a whole, the board, and perhaps other key member leaders. They should include the preferred:

- Vehicles for communication—teleconferences, emails or texts, written communications, or in-person meetings;
- Frequency—weekly, monthly, quarterly, or as needed; and
- Level of detail relative to verbal and written reporting.

The protocols will certainly be different depending on the type of relationship the CEO needs to have with each stakeholder—perhaps weekly teleconference updates with the chair as opposed to quarterly written reports to the board as a whole.

The board and CEO must also reach consensus about how various issues are communicated and to whom, including the following situations:

- A board member needs information or general assistance—typically provided to any member of the association.
- A board member needs information or assistance specific to her/his role as a board member.
- A board member has a concern that needs to be addressed or receives a complaint from a member.
- A board member has an idea for a new product, program, or service or receives a suggestion from a rank-and-file association member.

Jump Start the Chair/CEO Working Relationship

More likely than not, the new CEO will enter the association with the chair mid-way through her/his one-year tenure of office. With minimal previous interactions other than sitting across the table during one or more search committee meetings, there is precious little time for these two key individuals to forge a solid working relationship.

Ideally the chair and CEO will block out a day or two early on to get to know each other better, discuss hopes and expectations for the working relationship, and identify opportunities to support each other. ASAE sponsors two distinct programs that are helpful in this regard—the Symposium for Chief Executive & Chief Elected Officers and the Exceptional Boards workshop. Both programs are offered multiple times in any given year. Among other topics, they address the fundamentals of a strong volunteer/staff partnership, leadership styles, strategies to strengthen relationships, and enhancing board performance.

Given the popularity of these programs, it may be best to book a session shortly after the CEO search process begins, timed in line with the expected start date of the new CEO. If participation in one of these specific symposiums is impossible, other leadership retreats can be considered. Alternatively, the chair and CEO can craft their own agenda for a one- or two-day orientation at the chair's place of business or other setting.

Clarify Board/Staff Relationship Protocols

Board members, as well as other member leaders, tend to have more interactions with staff below the CEO level than what are experienced in corporate entities. Working relationships grow and frequently evolve into true friendships by the time a member works her/his way through the committee structure and into a board slot. Although strong board/staff relationships can be helpful, they may become dangerous. Friendships between individual board and staff members can serve to limit the CEO's ability to manage staff performance, including disciplining a board-favorite staff member when such discipline is needed.

With this in mind, from the very start of the new CEO's tenure there should be board/CEO consensus regarding the nature and limitations of board/staff interactions. Many CEOs will want to limit the extent to which board members socialize with staff outside association-sponsored events, including private dinners, staying at the homes of staff, or vacationing together. Limitations also may be placed on the extent to which board members elicit perceptions from individual staff members regarding staff morale or the strengths and weaknesses of individual staff members. This topic is addressed further in Chapter 6.

Establish Initial Performance Expectations

The next chapter will cover CEO performance management in far greater detail, including the articulation of performance metrics and objectives at the start of each year. For the first year, the CEO and board should agree on a set of quantifiable performance expectations for the first three months, six months, and year's end. By ensuring formal check-ins at these intervals, even if they involve only a telephone conversation between the chair and CEO, problems and concerns can be addressed before they become severe.

And the Buck Stops With...

The search committee chair bears the responsibility relative to the selection process. This key role is best filled by a current board officer who has a solid grasp of the association's operating environment, including board dynamics, and is viewed with respect and authority by her/his colleagues. It is typically the chair-elect or immediate past chair. The current board chair is usually not the best person for the role, given the numerous other responsibilities assigned to that position.

The search committee chair certainly should be a consensus builder but also needs to ferret out the silent dissenters. He/she needs to ensure all viewpoints are brought to the table and considered, especially in finalizing the position profile. The chair also needs to partner closely with search firm professionals and serve as an enforcer relative to recommended process steps and protocols. This includes the imperative for confidentiality of committee deliberations.

The board chair should take the lead when the CEO has been selected, leading her/his board colleagues in defining an appropriate CEO compensation strategy, defining initial performance expectations, and ensuring board members' support and involvement in effectively onboarding the new CEO.

The board chair will need to play a bigger role in the day-to-day operations of the association during the transition period, including interactions with staff, even with a solid interim CEO in place. Specifically, the chair will need to quickly orient the interim CEO to her/his expected role, including the extent of stakeholder assessments to be undertaken and changes that should or should not be made. It will also be helpful for staff to perceive that the board, and especially its chair, cares about them during a time when they may feel very vulnerable about their future with the organization.

Finally, the incoming CEO has a leadership role to play relative to her/his own onboarding. In addition to guidance provided in this chapter, there are many resources available through ASAE and elsewhere addressing best practices for CEO leadership during the initial days, months, and year. Ideally the CEO will already have in place a kitchen cabinet of colleague association CEOs with whom he/she can discuss challenges and ideas during these early days. It may also be helpful for the CEO to establish, with help from the transition team, a second kitchen cabinet of key leaders from the profession or trade who are not currently serving on the board.

The very demonstration of a proactive interest in onboarding by the CEO will generally be perceived positively by the board and should contribute to an aura of good feelings, the honeymoon that all new CEOs hope to experience.

Tying It Back to the Members

CEO transition can be extremely costly. In addition to and perhaps more important than out-of-pocket costs, is the lost organizational momentum that competitors can take advantage of. When an association board and its search committee shortchange the ideal search process or do not pay sufficient attention to new CEO onboarding, there is a high probability the new CEO will not be the right fit for the job or the board/CEO working relationship will not take hold. Then the association will find itself going through the search process all over again a few short years down the road.

Conversely, an upfront investment of time and resources to undertake the right search and onboarding processes will significantly increase the probability the association will have a CEO who is well positioned to address the current and future needs of the organization, with a long CEO/board honeymoon followed by many years of productive working relationships.

CHAPTER 5

Nurture the CEO/Board Working Relationship

THE CEO/BOARD HONEYMOON, WHETHER IT lasts a few months or a year or more, is now over. The CEO is fully oriented and up to speed with her/his new role and is starting to make an impact on the organization. Meanwhile, with each passing year, a few more of the board leaders who were responsible for the CEO's hiring transition out of their leadership roles. It is not too long before the entire crop of board leaders is different from the ones encountered by the CEO when he/she was hired.

With this change comes danger. The new board leaders may or may not have the same vested interest in the CEO's success, given they were not part of the hiring decision. It's even more dangerous if these new leaders represent a different political faction of the board than most members of the search committee.

Consider the following two scenarios.

> In Association A, the CEO enjoyed many years of what appeared to be a prolonged honeymoon. The organization was humming on all cylinders. There was significant growth in membership and nondues revenue, operational improvements affecting nearly every department, strong member satisfaction scores, and a healthy staff work environment that resulted in recognition by an external rating entity as an "employer of choice" environment.
>
> The CEO, confident in his success as a leader, did not see the warning signs. Although he had strong working relationships, extending to true friendships, with board officers in the early years, over time he in essence became lazy. He did not cultivate and nurture strong relationships with

succeeding generations of board leaders, instead resting on his laurels relative to traditional performance metrics. The upshot? In spite of his otherwise stellar performance, board politics caught up with this CEO, and much to his surprise, his contract was not renewed.

On the other hand, Association B's CEO knew she was hired to be a change agent charged with transforming what in essence was a club into a true professional society. She was also charged with changing the organization's strategic focus from domestic to international growth and reach. She set about her task and within two years had implemented a plethora of governance and operational best practices. She also made huge strides on the international front, teaming with member leaders to build relationships with comparable societies that resulted in several signed memorandums of understanding.

All was going well. Or so she thought. What she did not realize was that despite a façade of friendliness and good relationships with virtually all board members and officers during board meetings and retreats, there was discontent brewing under the surface. Many of the board members wanted their "club" back, and many others chafed at the increased international focus.

The CEO did her best to nurture relationships with the officers and other board members, including semiannual individual requests to every officer and board member for check-in meetings or teleconferences. However, perhaps because they were too busy or more likely because they preferred to avoid confrontation, most board members chose not to participate in such dialogues. Perhaps most alarming, the chair rejected the CEO's request for weekly update teleconferences, preferring instead to limit all CEO/chair interactions to scheduled executive committee and board meetings.

Without frequent contact and the opportunity to truly build working relationships, the CEO did not perceive the growing dissatisfaction with her leadership role, in spite of basically accomplishing what she was originally charged to do. Imagine her surprise when she was called into a meeting with the chair toward the end of his term and handed her walking papers.

Both these situations could have been avoided if the board and CEO had truly prioritized their working relationship. There are too many similar scenarios in the association world, with what could have been—should have been—long-term and productive CEO/board partnerships that were cut short to the detriment of the association and its members, throwing the organization into turmoil and stagnation as the process to select a new staff leader begins yet again.

For the Good of the Members

There are two distinct elements to the CEO/board working relationship—the formal and the informal. Both are important, not just for the individuals involved but for the success of the association. The formal aspect addresses the nuts and bolts of a board's managing the CEO's performance. It also includes expectations for decision-making roles and communication protocols (i.e., face-to-face, telephonic, and written communications between the CEO, various officers, and the board as a whole). The chair and her/his board colleagues need to take the lead role, and are ultimately accountable for success in execution.

Conversely, the CEO is typically best positioned to take the lead role with informal relationship building. This involves getting to know each board member and officer well, including her/his personality, abilities, and preferences, and developing mutual appreciation, respect, and synergy in the CEO's interactions with each of them as individuals. Some CEOs make the mistake of believing such relationship building is unimportant, and focus on meeting or exceeding expectations of quantifiable performance. These same CEOs usually find themselves scratching their heads in disbelief when their employment agreements are not renewed in spite of otherwise stellar performance.

Treat Performance Management Seriously

Very few of us enjoy the formalities associated with staff performance management, whether in the supervisor or subordinate role. It takes time away from addressing overwhelming workloads and the day-to-day unexpected fires we need to put out. It is also very uncomfortable, if not mentally and emotionally exhausting, to be on either the giving or receiving end when there are performance issues that need to be addressed. No wonder that it frequently takes human resources department staff so much time and effort to ensure that supervisors complete performance planning and assessment forms and that formal supervisor/subordinate dialogues take place.

Even if distasteful, adhering to a comprehensive performance management process is critical—all the more so for a position as important as the CEO's. Doing so will help ensure the CEO is prioritizing time and other resources of the staff on what the board deems to be most critical.

The process should include the following components, ideally corresponding with the association's fiscal year.

Performance Planning

Everyone deserves to know at the start of any given year how he/she will be assessed at the end of the year. This is not only a matter of being fair to the CEO. It is also the right thing to do for the organization and its success.

Many CEO performance management systems focus exclusively on the job description, with the CEO assessed on selected roles and accountabilities. Although the job description is certainly important, performance assessment should be multidimensional. It is not only important to assess what is accomplished, but how it is accomplished. The "what" should be quantitative and measurable. The "how" is typically measured subjectively, but should be based on predefined criteria.

More specifically, following are definitions of performance planning and assessment components that will be subsequently mentioned and discussed.

- *Metrics:* A quantitative component that addresses ongoing responsibilities of an organization, department, or position. There is an expectation that these responsibilities will remain relatively consistent from year to year unless there are significant changes in the operating environment or strategic direction. However, the targeted levels of performance may change, typically becoming more stringent and aggressive with the passing of time.
- *Objectives:* Another quantitative component representing one-time targeted accomplishments for an organization, department, or position. Objectives should be closely tied to the organization's current strategic and operating priorities. Although the anticipated time frame to complete a given objective may extend for several years (e.g., implementation of a new technology platform), there should be predetermined performance milestones along the way, enabling the board to assess whether or not appropriate progress is being made.
- *Competencies:* These represent a combination of practical and theoretical knowledge, skills, behaviors, attributes, and values demonstrated by an organization, department, or individual. Although some human resources professionals advocate that competency performance can be quantified, realistically it takes more time and other resources to do than most organizations want to expend. As a result, most organizations ask supervisors, in this case the board for the CEO, to assess competencies based on examples and impressions.

In undertaking performance planning, the quantifiable components (i.e., metrics and objectives) should be developed utilizing the SMART acronym—Specific, Measurable, Attainable, Relevant to higher-level objectives, typically based on the strategic plan for the CEO position, and Time-defined. Ideally, three predetermined performance levels should be identified for each one:

- *Threshold:* Below which performance is unacceptable;
- *Target:* Representing solid, at expectation performance; and
- *Superior:* Indicative of exemplary performance.

By identifying three levels of performance, there actually will be five levels of ultimate performance that can be used to assess the CEO, including performance that is below threshold and performance that is above superior.

Appendix 5.1 presents a sample format for documenting CEO metrics and objectives during the planning process. Note that it includes identification of the measurement approach that will be used at the end of the year for each item, along with the weight assigned by the board to each metric and objective. The CEO should be asked to take a first pass at defining metrics and objectives before the start of each year, with the board editing and approving the final set shortly thereafter.

Appendix 5.2 presents a set of CEO competencies that have been used for several association CEOs, including myself. Even though competency performance will be assessed subjectively by most boards, it is important for the CEO to understand at the start of the year what competencies will be evaluated so he or she can keep them in mind as the year progresses.

Midyear Assessment

A CEO's performance, even if actions and behaviors are consistent over time, may be viewed differently from year to year by her/his primary supervisors, the chair and other officers, because the officer incumbents typically change each year. What one year may be perceived as appropriate or even exemplary performance may the next year be viewed as annoying or unacceptable. With this in mind, the CEO should initiate informal check-ins with the chair and other officers throughout the year regarding her/his working relationships with them and performance in the CEO role. However, it is a good idea to have a more formal performance check-in midyear.

During the midyear check-in, the CEO should take the lead in updating the officers regarding performance on CEO metrics and objectives established at the beginning of the year. If there have been significant changes in organizational priorities or the operating environment, the CEO or officers may legitimately request that specific metrics or objectives be added, deleted, or changed relative to performance targets or weight assignments. Such adjustments should receive full-board approval.

The chair should gather and present to the CEO feedback from the officer group regarding performance on CEO competencies. If any concerns are raised, the chair should ideally provide suggestions for how best to address them.

In addition to discussing metrics, objectives, and competencies, any CEO would benefit from receiving feedback to the following questions:

1. What should the CEO be doing moref?
2. What should the CEO be doing less?
3. What should the CEO continue doing?

Having such a midyear dialogue will give the CEO an opportunity to adjust her/his approach to leadership with each unique officer group before working relationships suffer to the point of negatively affecting the organization.

Year-End Assessment

The process for year-end CEO performance assessment usually should mimic what applies to any employee, with both written and verbal components, along with active participation by both the employee and her/his supervisor. The biggest difference and challenge is that the CEO does not have one supervisor, but rather nine, fifteen, or more. Regardless of the number of board members, each one has a fiduciary duty to contribute to the process, even if only affirming a performance assessment prepared by one or more board colleagues.

Following is one step-by-step model to consider. Modifications should be made to fit your unique operating environment.

Competency Performance Assessment—Target Completion Within 30 Days of Year End

1. By the end of the performance year, the CEO submits to the chair her/his self-assessment of competencies, using a form that was finalized and agreed on by all parties at the start of the year. The form should include opportunities for both numerical ratings and commentary in support of numerical ratings.
2. The chair asks all board members who served in that capacity during most or all of the previous year to complete the same assessment form rating the CEO's performance. Board members should be encouraged to assign ratings to competencies only if they have personal knowledge

or experience regarding the CEO's performance, leaving ratings for other competencies blank.

The chair may elect to distribute the CEO's self-assessment to board members prior to this step. Doing so may be helpful in reminding board members of actions, documented in the self-assessment, which they would have otherwise not known about or perhaps forgotten. On the flip side, it is human nature for the CEO in her/his self-assessment to focus on the positive, thereby providing a somewhat biased frame of reference as board members complete their assessments of the CEO.

3. The chair accumulates and averages competency rating scores from all board members, inputting the average results for each competency on the assessment form along with a synopsis of key themes from narrative comments. Individual competency average scores are averaged to arrive at an overall average competency assessment.
4. The chair presents the final competency assessment ratings and narrative input, as documented on the performance assessment form, to the board for approval.

Metric/Objective Performance Assessment—Target Completion Within 45 Days of Year's End

It typically takes longer to assess metric/objective performance because performance data applicable to Step 1 may not be available until two or three weeks after the year ends.

1. The CEO gathers performance data pertaining to each metric and objective, using pre-determined methodology (e.g., financial statements prepared by the CFO), to arrive at a numerical rating for each one. These are documented on the performance assessment form. If applicable, the CEO will supply commentary identifying roadblocks and other extenuating circumstances that affected achieved performance.
2. The chair, or other designated board members, independently verify the CEO's self-assessment of selected or all metrics and objectives. For example, the CFO may be consulted relative to financial performance and the IT director may be consulted relative to the achievement of technology milestones. In small organizations, where the CEO fills all key administrative roles, the board may need to rely on its own members, or perhaps a past board member, to undertake an audit of metric and objective performance, using whatever performance data may be available.

3. If there are discrepancies between the CEO's assessments of metric and objective performance and those gathered through this review process, the chair or officers discuss(es) these with the CEO before finalizing the ratings that will be presented to the board.
4. The chair presents the final metric/objective assessment ratings and narrative input, as documented on the performance assessment form, to the board for approval.

Performance Discussion—Target Completion Within 60 Days of Year's End
The CEO deserves to hear in person, face-to-face, the board-approved assessment of her/his performance. The now past chair facilitates the dialogue, ideally joined by phone or in person by one or more board colleagues, perhaps this year's chair or this year's executive committee.

Assuming the steps outlined above have been followed (i.e., performance planning at the beginning of the year, a midyear assessment, and periodic informal check-ins during the rest of the year), there should be few surprises for the CEO. The conversation will be cordial, if not mostly pleasant, as accomplishments are highlighted and recognized.

However, as with any other employee, there are nearly always opportunities for the CEO to improve performance. These should be conveyed and discussed in a straightforward, unemotional manner. Ideally the board representatives will be prepared to share specific ideas for the CEO to consider in attaining expected or better performance. If there are significant performance deficits, the board representatives should consult with external legal counsel to strategize how these will be conveyed and the extent to which a formal performance improvement plan may be required.

Compensation Implications

The final ingredient of effective CEO performance management is its effect on compensation. The previous chapter discussed the importance of defining the competitive market for CEO compensation as well as the need to decide how total compensation will be targeted relative to the defined market. A key strategic question is how strong the ties will be between CEO performance and compensation.

Such ties can certainly be reinforced by annual base salary adjustments. For example, the board may convey to the CEO at the start of the year that a year-end overall performance assessment of 2 on a 5-point scale will result in no salary increase the next year, a 3 will carry a 2 percent increase, and a 4 a 5 percent increase.

However, the greater opportunity to recognize performance deemed most critical by the board and association lies with the use of incentive compensation. In this regard associations, similar to most nonprofits, lag behind their corporate brethren. In the corporate world it is not at all unusual for CEOs to have 50 percent or more of their total compensation at risk based on achieving a combination of one-year and multiyear predefined performance targets, utilizing a combination of cash and equity. Conversely, recent ASAE compensation survey results indicate roughly half of association CEOs do not have the opportunity to receive incentive compensation. Even for those eligible, it is rare to find incentive compensation targeted at more than 10 percent of base salary.

Design of a structurally sound, highly motivating CEO incentive compensation plan that reinforces performance desired by the board is beyond the scope of this book. It is best to engage consulting professionals in tailoring an approach for your association. However, key design principles include the following:

- Tie most, if not all, incentive compensation to the achievement of quantifiable results (i.e., metrics and objectives developed during performance planning), minimizing subjectivity.
- Define award possibilities at the start of the performance period and communicate these to the CEO. For example, if the weighted average tally of metric and objective performance is at:
  - Threshold, an award of 5 percent of base salary will be generated.
  - Target, an award of 10 percent of base salary will be generated.
  - Superior, an award of 20 percent of base salary will be generated.

Regardless of how performance and compensation are tied together, the key is that strategic thinking guides decision making, as opposed to the board making haphazard, seat-of-the-pants compensation adjustments.

Stick to Agreed Roles

In Chapter 2 considerable attention was given to defining appropriate roles for officers, governance entities, and staff and mitigating the propensity of officers and governance entities to insert themselves in domains that are typically best performed by staff. Without rehashing in detail here, it is important to reinforce that the health of working relationships between the CEO, officers, and other board members depends on all parties adherence to guidelines that have been established, using the previously discussed role matrices as guides. When new situations arise that require decision making not addressed in these guidelines, they should be discussed openly and collaboratively with all relevant stakeholders and the guidelines amended if necessary.

Follow the Golden Rule in Communication

The presence or lack of open, transparent communication built on a foundation of trust and mutual respect is a key determinant of how successful the CEO/board working relationship will be. Unfortunately, for some individuals knowledge means power, and they may withhold information, creating guarded, strained communications.

The previous chapter addressed the need for the board and a new CEO to define up front basic communication protocols. However, beyond these basic formalities, there remains a need to address and reinforce the importance of communication in the day-to-day board/CEO working relationship.

Board Communication With the CEO

Board officers and other board members should adopt the mindset that the CEO is a colleague, entitled to the same level of communication they receive. The only exception is discussions regarding the CEO's performance, and even here the CEO should receive timely, candid feedback if there are performance concerns.

With this in mind, all in-person, phone, and email conversations involving the full board or the executive committee should include the CEO. The same should hold true relative to sharing documents and other information among board members. If/when the board goes into executive session to discuss sensitive issues, the CEO should be included as a full participant.

It is easy to overlook the informal aspect of communication, including spur-of-the-moment conversations that take place in a bar, over dinner, or other social gatherings of board members. Such conversations can easily migrate from casual to substantial relative to association business. If the CEO is not present (he/she should be invited and attends most such gatherings), it is important that those involved in the conversation be mindful of what it may be helpful for the CEO to know based on such discussions.

CEO Communications with the Board

All CEOs face the challenge of determining where to draw the line in terms of what is communicated to officers and the full board. So much is going on within an organization at any given moment of time! Communicating too much can easily overwhelm board members, causing them to gloss over all communications, including key information they truly need to pay attention to. Communicating too much, especially with regard to operational issues, can also serve as a springboard to getting board members involved in operational decision making. As one CEO put it, "Give someone a problem, and they'll solve it for you."

On the other hand, if a CEO severely limits what is communicated to the board, he/she may be perceived as controlling, and perhaps even disdainful of the board's fiduciary role in looking out for the best interests of the organization and its members. Lack of communication may result in unpleasant surprises if board members are confronted by a member, or worse yet someone from outside the association, with a request to respond to a piece of "news" that they did not know. Such situations can easily escalate to broken trust with the CEO.

To avoid perceptions of communicating too much or too little, association CEOs should continually experiment and tweak the level of detail provided, format, and frequency of communication to the board and its officers. They should elicit feedback from the board at least semiannually, if not more frequently, regarding their satisfaction. Communication should also be a key topic of conversation between the CEO and the chair at the start of the chair's term, given varying communication preferences from one chair to another.

Realizing there is no single best approach to CEO-generated communication, it still may be helpful to heed advice offered by various long-term association CEOs.

> From Arlene Pietranton, CEO of the American Speech-Language-Hearing Association, Rockville, Maryland: "Association CEOs need to understand the key role they play as curators of information for the board and its members, given the deluge of information that is out there. As curators, they also need to be attuned to patterns of communication and how people want to access information. This includes giving more attention to social media as a vehicle to convey information and receive feedback."

> From Liz Lucas, Executive Director & CEO of Soroptimist International of the Americas, Philadelphia, Pennsylvania: "Use a performance dashboard to define success and communicate progress to the board on a monthly basis. Board/CEO collaboration in developing the dashboard assures that everyone is on the same page relative to what is important to track and what to be informed about. The dashboard is also succinct, making it quick and relatively easy for a board member to stay appropriately updated on the association's progress, or lack thereof."

> From Paul Pomerantz, CEO of the American Society of Anesthesiologists, Schaumburg, Illinois: "Communicate, communicate, communicate! I have found it very helpful to send a weekly report of highlights to the board—the

good, the bad, and the ugly. The report takes no more than an hour or two to write and is limited to two pages. The board loves it because it keeps them appropriately informed and avoids surprises, which is very important."

From Dean Wilkerson, Executive Director of The American College of Emergency Physicians, Irving, Texas: "I have used several different approaches over time to communicate with our officers, but I have found that what works best is to include the top officers (in our case the immediate past president, president, and president-elect) in weekly update teleconferences. Doing so helps ensure there are no surprises among us regarding what we're thinking about key issues. It promotes transparency and trust building, and also is good in terms of leadership continuity, with the president-elect benefiting from hearing how his predecessors interact with me and I with them—openly, candidly, and respectfully."

Nurture Individual Relationships

The Association A case study presented at the start of this chapter conveys what can happen when an otherwise high-performing CEO ignores relationship building with the board. Extending this case study further, the successor to this CEO was in many ways the polar opposite. In considering traditional measures of performance, including financial results and membership growth, his track record was poor. This CEO also quickly garnered a reputation for being a horrible staff leader, resulting in significant undesirable staff turnover, poor morale for those who remained, and a bad reputation as an employer within the local association community. Yet, this CEO understood the importance of relationship building with his board and was a master at nurturing individual working relationships. This included giving extra attention to the rising stars, individuals who ultimately would be the most influential decision makers on the board.

The result? In spite of widespread discontent among association members and staff regarding the CEO, a fraction of which would have led to quick termination of the previous CEO, the board was reluctant to terminate this CEO, their friend, who continued to serve many years in the role.

The lesson here is not for the CEO to ignore organizational performance and focus primarily on board relationship building. Rather, the lesson is the importance of both performance and relationship building to the long-term success of the board/CEO working relationship. As indicated previously, the CEO has primary responsibility for relationship building. Board members ideally will be receptive to the CEO's overtures, although they also need to place boundaries on the relationship to ensure they have the necessary fortitude to make tough decisions relative to CEO discipline and retention if necessary.

CEO/board relationships are built over time. In most, if not all cases, the CEO will have some level of familiarity with board members before their beginning service on the board, perhaps through the members' involvement in committee work or other lower-level leadership roles. If the CEO has good intuition and is attuned to rising stars—the individuals most likely to someday become her/his boss on the board—he/she will be wise to not only pay attention to such individuals but start nurturing relationships with them. What makes them tick? What core strengths do they bring to the table? What developmental needs do they have, and is there an opportunity for the CEO to serve as a sounding board or in a coaching capacity? Even a few casual, encouraging conversations during the annual meeting or after a committee meeting can go a long way toward building camaraderie.

If the newly elected board member is a surprise, the learning curve for the CEO will be steeper, but it is still possible to quickly forge solid relationships if the CEO takes time to jump start the process. Following are some tips for approaching individual relationship building at each level of board leadership.

Board Members

Once the decision has been made and announced that someone will be joining the board, the CEO should undertake research to become more familiar with the individual. Ideally this will include accessing information provided to the Nominating Committee by the then-candidate, along with promotional and campaign material that may have been generated during the election cycle that speaks to the candidate's interests, priorities, and perhaps tidbits about his/her family and hobbies. Much can also be gleaned from reviewing the new board member's LinkedIn profile and other information available from an internet search.

The CEO should be among the first individuals to reach out and congratulate each new board member, perhaps including a gift from the headquarters office. I have found it helpful to schedule introductory telephone calls with each new board member, during which I have asked the following questions:

1. What are you most proud about up to this point in terms of your involvement with this association?
2. What role do you hope to play on the board and what strengths do you bring to the table?

3. What concerns, if any, do you have about serving effectively on the board? What type of coaching, if any, would you like to receive from me, your board colleagues, or others to become as good a board member as possible?
4. In what other ways can we help transition you to your new role?
5. What topics would you like to see addressed and emphasized during board orientation?
6. What are your hopes for the association's future direction?
7. Do you have any current impressions regarding how the association should address _____ ? (Pick a few key strategic issues you know the board will be grappling with.)
8. From your perspective, how are things going with regard to the association's products, programs, and services? What is going well and what needs to be improved?
9. What are your impressions of the headquarters staff regarding our service to the association, its members, and you personally?
10. What guidelines should I and other staff use in terms of communicating with you?
    - Do you prefer telephone calls or email?
    - If the preference is for telephone calls, and we cannot reach you, should we leave voice mails, ask to talk with your assistant, or resort to email?
    - What time of day works best for you—early mornings, traditional working hours, nights and weekends, or any time?
11. Is there anything else, professional or personal, that you think it would be helpful for me to know about you?

Ideally this conversation will be a two-way street, with the CEO being asked corresponding questions and willingly sharing his/her thoughts, preferences, ideas, and details of life outside of work.

Beyond this introduction, the CEO should be actively engaged with new board members throughout the more formal orientation process, taking advantage of meeting breaks and social events to have informal discussions and check-ins regarding how the process is being perceived.

I have found it helpful to schedule semiannual follow-up check-ins throughout the board member's tenure to ensure impressions remain positive relative to the organization, staff, governance structure and operation, and working relationships with board colleagues and the CEO.

The CEO can use such feedback to address any concerns that arise. In addition to asking many of the same questions identified above, it is important to hear directly from board members how satisfied they are with the roles they are playing on the board. Are there any governance issues they believe need to be addressed or questions the CEO can answer? Are there any changes they would like to see considered relative to how the CEO or other staff can better support the association and the board member personally?

Aside from scheduled interactions, Paul Pomerantz counsels, "Although it's not always easy or enjoyable to do, the CEO should engage as much as possible and develop more informal personal relationships with every board member, even those he/she may not personally like. This can be accomplished throughout the year during breaks of board meetings, social functions at the annual meeting, and elsewhere. Even if good friendships do not always result, the conversations and information that is shared back and forth will typically build trust and appreciation that will have a positive impact in the board room and other formal CEO/board interactions."

Taking this a step further, several CEOs make it a practice of being mindful in their travel plans of board members living nearby travel destinations, inviting such members if possible for coffee or a meal. Conversely, they can offer all board members the opportunity to meet if the board members' travels take them to the headquarters city. Such get-togethers can lead to more in-depth conversations and relationship building than would otherwise be possible.

Officers Not in the Chair Progression

An association's secretary, treasurer, vice-president, and other officer positions frequently represent crucial steps for a member's ascent up the leadership structure. Each one can serve as a leadership testing ground that grooms him/her for a possible chair-elect role in the future. The individual in such a role may or may not have a wealth of previous experience to draw on (e.g., a treasurer who does not have a finance background). Even with a sound officer-specific orientation program in place, any officer will typically appreciate the CEO's checking in with him/her more regularly than previously (at least quarterly) to ensure all is well and provide coaching if desired. Such check-ins will also give the CEO on opportunity to better assess how this individual might perform in the chair-elect and chair roles and the type of working relationship that can be expected a year or two down the road.

Chair-Elect

Once a member leader is formally identified as the chair-elect, the CEO should ratchet up interactions with and subsequent understanding of the individual. What type of leader will he/she be in the chair role? Which chair duties will be easy for the individual to perform and which will be a struggle, or ones the individual would prefer to delegate? Is there an opportunity for the CEO to provide coaching to the chair-elect in this regard before the chair year begins?

The chair-elect year can be the ideal time frame for that individual and the CEO to attend one of the ASAE board/staff leader programs mentioned previously. In addition to or in place of attending such a program, many CEOs make it a practice to visit the chair-elect in his/her work environment, and in some cases spend time with their family, to garner a better understanding of issues and challenges faced by the individual outside of the association.

Lucas recommends that such an intensive CEO/chair-elect get-acquainted experience take place within the first three months of the chair-elect's term. She then uses a structured approach over the next nine months, including in-depth teleconferences every three months, to build the working relationship, uncover nuances in leadership style and preferences, identify coaching needs, and in other ways prepare the individual to easily transition into the chair role.

Richard Yep, CEO of the American Counseling Association, Alexandria, Virginia, stresses the importance of finding common ground during this time period: "Even if the chair-elect and CEO have completely different life experiences, personalities, and priorities, they can always find something in common. Both individuals should look for and embrace these commonalities, using them to build a friendship and working relationship."

Chair

In most associations the CEO is accountable to the entire board, and the board collectively makes decisions relative to retention, termination, performance assessment and management, and compensation adjustments. However, the chair typically fulfills the role of day-to-day supervisor to the CEO, and in many associations the board takes its lead in making decisions from this individual. In other words, the chair's relationship with the CEO can hold a large sway on how remaining board members view the CEO. In extreme cases, generally positive feelings toward the CEO can turn literally overnight into concerns and friction based on what the chair conveys to board colleagues and can ultimately lead to the CEO's exiting the organization.

Consequently, the importance of the chair/CEO working relationship cannot be overemphasized. Both individuals should commit to developing the relationship to its best and fullest extent beginning well before the chair takes office. Regardless of how well the working relationship has been previously developed, it is helpful for the incoming chair and CEO to meet within the month preceding the leadership change to clarify desires and expectations for the working relationship. Appendix 5.3 includes a set of questions that can serve as a starting point for the CEO in framing this dialogue. It includes a number of get-to-know-you questions that ideally have been answered long before.

If the CEO has been diligent in undertaking the types of relationship building proposed above, extending as far back as the chair's pre-board involvement and leadership experiences, and assuming the chair has been appropriately receptive to such overtures, the chair/CEO working relationship should be well-positioned to be solid and productive from Day 1. All that remains is for these two individuals to ensure they prioritize the relationship enough to:

- Talk at least biweekly, even if for only a quick, informal check-in. Exhibit 5.1 provides a framework for such discussions, focusing on action items the chair needs to address as well as informational items;
- Communicate respectfully, openly, and candidly on key association issues, taking the approach of "what I would like or need to know if our roles were reversed;"
- Not surprising each other during board meetings or other formal association meetings, previewing anything that might be viewed as a surprise in advance; and
- Seek opportunities to build each other up in the eyes of other board members, the general membership, and external stakeholders.

And the Buck Stops With...

The board chair is responsible for the execution of a multifaceted CEO performance management and compensation program. This includes performance planning, midyear assessment, year-end assessment, and compensation adjustments.

The chair and CEO have joint accountability for ensuring that predetermined decision-making roles and communication protocols are followed, the chair serving as enforcer for the board and the CEO as enforcer for staff.

Although informal relationship building should be a two-way street, with both parties prioritizing its development and demonstrating receptivity, realistically the CEO is best positioned to be the primary initiator and driver over time as association members progress through the leadership structure.

Tying It Back to the Members

This book has devoted considerable space to the board's fiduciary duties relative to:

- CEO selection and onboarding;
- Performance management, and other interactions with the CEO; and
- The CEO's role in forging a close working relationship with member leaders.

This level of attention speaks to the significant impact that the right CEO and a strong board/CEO working relationship can have on the association and its members. The positive energy extends well beyond the board room, permeating the staff organization and perceived by corporate and advocacy partners, current members, and target members. The case studies presented at the end of this book highlight the tremendous accomplishments that can be attained in large part because of the board/CEO dynamic.

Conversely, I have personally witnessed and heard war stories from peer CEOs of associations that never seem to get it right, due to the actions of their boards. Some associations experience a revolving door of CEOs accompanied by poor board/CEO working relationships that jeopardize progress on strategic initiatives and collaboration opportunities with external entities. This takes time and attention away from adding member value and serving members and, ultimately, places the association at risk relative to competitors.

Chair/CEO Biweekly Update Month/Day/Year

Action Items From Previous Biweekly Update

[EXAMPLE] **International Strategy Development:** Following up on our previous discussions, we need to decide soon relative to FY1X leader/staff travel to key international meetings. Specifically, I propose you select one or more board members to serve as our association's representatives to the ABC September meeting in South Korea and the PQR November meeting in Israel. I anticipate accompanying the leader(s) to both meetings, and we should consider exhibiting there. Are you comfortable planning and budgeting along those lines? Are there other international meetings you believe board leaders and I should plan on attending in FY1X?

New Action Items

[EXAMPLE] **Spring Leadership Conference Special Guests:** As planning continues for the conference, we're wondering if you anticipate inviting any special guests to New Orleans? If so, please let me know who they are and if you need assistance with travel logistics.

FYI Items

[EXAMPLE] **IT Platform Implementation Update:** We have started the contract negotiation stage for our selected AMS, LMS, and CMS vendors. We're hoping to have final agreements inked by the end of March, with implementation on the CMS ideally commencing by mid-March.

[EXAMPLE] **New Marketing Director:** Jane Doe joined the staff this week after serving more than five years with me in a similar capacity at another association.

Known CEO Days out of the Office: I will be out of the office the following days:

- February 28–March 1: Washington Committee meeting
- March 4–5: Vacation in Colorado

• • •

CHAPTER 6

Strive for Win/Win Stakeholder Relationships

"Alone we can do so little. Together we can do so much."
– Helen Keller

PERHAPS THE BIGGEST ADVANTAGE AN association has over its competitors, especially those in the corporate world, is the vast army of individuals and organizations that have a vested interest in its success. Most of an association's customers are also members. Many of these members are passionate about the association's vision and mission and stand ready to donate their time and intellectual capital to its success. The value of this free resource is immeasurable.

Aside from members, associations typically have a cadre of corporate partners—vendors, sponsors, exhibitors, advertisers, grant makers, and affinity partners. These partners certainly have their self-interests; however, they also realize that their success is affected by the association's success. Many corporations are eager to team with associations in creating and delivering value to members, including educational content, or to donate to an association's foundation with few strings attached.

For associations engaged in advocacy, there is a third stakeholder group composed of current and potential organizational allies. Realistically, even associations with multimillion dollar budget political action committees need such allies to influence legislators and regulators.

Last, but not least, is staff. This stakeholder group includes individuals with experience and expertise in each functional area that is critical to the association's success. Although some staff are there just for the money, in every association I have served the vast majority are passionate supporters of the association and the members they serve.

All of these stakeholders—members, corporate and advocacy partners, and staff—are critical to an association's success. Yet, in many cases very little board member attention and meeting agenda time is devoted to ensuring that relationships with these stakeholders are strong and productive.

What happens if your members perceive that their opinions are not valued or their expressed desires to become involved in the association's work are rebuffed? What happens when your corporate partners believe the association takes advantage of them and has no interest in their success? What happens when current and potential advocacy partners perceive your association has tunnel vision regarding its own regulatory and legislative agenda, unwilling to compromise or support what other organizations are trying to accomplish? And what happens when your staff hear board members bemoaning staff-driven organizations and experience the board adopting an "us versus them mentality," treating staff as mere pawns as opposed to partners?

The answer to all these questions is disengagement and unwillingness on the part of these stakeholders to devote their all to your association's success. Association board members and the CEO must assure this does not happen!

For the Good of the Members

Association leaders need to keep a pulse on stakeholders' perceptions and ensure a mindset of forging win/win working relationships. What is meant by win/win? Noted author and leadership guru Stephen Covey described the concept in his book *The 7 Habits of Highly Effective People:* "Win/win is a frame of mind and heart that constantly seeks mutual benefit in all human interactions. Win/win means that agreements or solutions are mutually beneficial, mutually satisfying. With a win/win solution, all parties feel good about the decision and feel committed to the action plan. Win/win sees life as a cooperative, not a competitive arena."

Understand Your Members

The most important stakeholder group association leaders should focus on is the members; without members the association would not exist. It starts with developing and maintaining a true understanding of who they are, what challenges and opportunities they face, and what they are looking for in their association.

Many associations' bylaws require board representation by various member segments and/or geographic regions. With this comes an assumption that these board representatives understand what members of their specific constituency want and can speak on their behalf. Is such an assumption valid? Not necessarily. It's really no different than assuming that a member of Congress, representing a specific geographic region, in all cases conveys opinions and votes according to the wishes of his/her constituents. We all know that is not the case!

I have witnessed numerous examples of board members asserting that "the members want this" only to be proven wrong by member research data that clearly contradict their point of view. Board members' perceptions compared to those of rank-and-file members are frequently as different as city dwellers and farmers. With few exceptions, board members have a long history of active engagement on committees and other leadership roles leading up to their board service. They also are typically much bigger consumers of the association's products, programs, and services. Their mindset is of the ultra-active member, which probably represents less than 5 percent of the association's total members. Try as they may to put themselves in the shoes of the remaining 95 percent, board members cannot do so without help.

This holds true even for the most networked board members. Their interactions are still limited to a relatively small percent of members they encounter in professional and social settings. They do not have the time or ability to personally interact with the vast majority of members that comprise the association. With this in mind, the board should be open to member feedback and comments and should support a continuous program of member research directed by staff or external contractors. This includes periodic member surveys, focus groups, and other tools to gather input from members. Time should be allocated periodically on board agendas to present and discuss the results of member research.

In addition to listening and reacting to what members say, it's also important for the board to consider what members actually do. Sheri Jacobs, in her book *The Art of Membership* (Jossey-Bass, 2014), says, "Asking your target audience about their preferences alone may not provide you with accurate information. You need to look at an individual's behavior as well.... Although preference questions may provide important data on how a member would act or respond when few or no barriers (such as cost or time) exist, they often do not reflect the realities most people and organizations face."

For example, member survey data may indicate a strong preference by members for an onsite as opposed to webinar educational program. But a subsequent analysis of actual attendance data may indicate sparse attendance for the onsite meeting contrasted by high attendance for the webinar. Much as they may prefer onsite education, the timing of course offerings may not match with job-related or personal priorities. Even if the timing is right, members may view the cost of such programs as excessive.

Finally, in terms of understanding members, board members and staff need to be cognizant of what members may not realize they want or need. Steve Jobs, putting aside his flaws in interacting with his staff and others, is the epitome of an innovator who understood what his customers would value in the future. He leveraged this understanding to build the huge corporate empire that Apple is today.

In the association world, there may not be a Steve Jobs equivalent. However, association leaders can gauge future needs by consulting with recognized futurists and by focusing a portion of member research on problems and challenges they currently face or anticipate facing in the future. Associations will also increasingly have the ability to mine demographic and other data in their association management systems, helping them build predictive models for what members will value in the future.

With a solid understanding of an association's members, the board will be well positioned to undertake strategic planning, a topic addressed further in Chapter 7. This planning includes identifying specific initiatives that current and future members will identify with and embrace.

Engage Your Members

Aside from understanding members, association leaders should make sure opportunities exist for members to engage with the association. The vast majority of most associations' members are mailbox members. Although they perceive value in your association, they do not want to engage other than opening the mailbox for their journals and magazines, extracting information from the members' only section of the association's website, and perhaps occasionally attending an annual meeting.

However, there is almost always a subset of members that truly wants to become involved in the association. In many cases the motivations are ego fulfillment and resumé padding. However, in many other cases the motivation is primarily altruistic, a passion for the association's mission and a desire to support it.

Regardless of motivation, involved members represent a huge potential resource for your association. Boards and CEOs should collaborate in identifying opportunities for members to serve. With a little creativity, small but meaningful roles can be identified. Such roles are an excellent entrée for members to "test the water" relative to association work.

Some associations use members as first-time-attendee ambassadors at their annual meeting, making sure that the newbies feel welcomed and oriented to all the meeting has to offer. Other associations offer members the opportunity to serve on focus groups. Others still, including the Heart Rhythm Society,Washington, DC, have a defined group of members that are on standby to serve as a sounding board when staff or the board needs input on various issues. More than 900 HRS members participate on its Advisory Panel, completing brief monthly surveys and receiving exclusive access to summary reports.

These relatively small roles may be all most members want to undertake. However, these assignments can be excellent opportunities to vet and prepare them for more substantive roles, including service on committees and work teams. Association boards and CEOs should ensure the committee/work team selection process is as open, fair, and inclusive as possible. Many associations rely too much on the good ole boy or girl network to fill vacant positions. Criteria for service on committees and work teams should be documented and readily available for any member to see. There should be open calls for members to apply for vacant positions, and the selection process should be fair. Limitations should be placed on how many committees a given member can serve on, assuming there are far more members interested in serving than there are available slots. Finally, there should be limitations on how long a member can serve on a specific entity, be it the board or a committee. As valuable as experience and historical perspective can be, any organizational entity benefits from a continual infusion of new blood and fresh perspectives.

In working with member stakeholders, association's leaders must focus on the definition of win/win, providing a good result for everyone involved. Your members need to feel appreciated, understood, and enabled to engage as they choose with your association. In other words, they need to feel the love! When members know they are valued, your member retention rates will be sky-high and your association will have an army of passionate volunteers to call on as needed.

Help Your Corporate Partners Achieve Their Goals

For most associations, financial support from corporate partners, including grants, sponsorships, exhibit revenue, advertising, and affinity programs, is critical for the organization's success. Such financial support contributes to the development and subsequent operation of products, programs, and services that individually may be unprofitable but are highly valued by members.

In addition to financial support, the corporate community can be a tremendous knowledge resource to associations. Corporate partner representatives can educate an association's members via the exhibit hall at annual meetings, advertising, or other means regarding new products and services that will directly benefit members in serving their own customers. In many instances corporate partners can also supplement an association's resources and expertise in developing and delivering new educational programs at meetings, online, or in print.

As valuable as corporate partners can be, when taken to an extreme, engagement with them can be detrimental to an organization. Some associations, in their desperation for more corporate dollars, give away too much real estate on their website and publications for corporate logos and promotional materials. They endorse questionable, unproven corporate products and in other ways dilute or tarnish the association's brand in favor of corporate branding.

One association I worked with gave a corporation branding rights for two key social events at the annual meeting. The annual meeting, in the eyes of many attendees, became a co-branded association/Company X offering. What a good deal that was for the corporate partner! For a relatively modest investment of time and money, the sponsor generated nearly as much goodwill from the association's members as the association did.

Keeping in mind both the positive and potentially detrimental aspects of corporate relations, association boards have a fiduciary duty to contribute to and ultimately approve the organization's corporate relations strategy. Strategic questions include the following:

- To what extent will specific industry segments or companies be prioritized or excluded relative to soliciting financial support?
- Will there be limitations regarding exhibit floor space that will be offered to various industry segments or general consumer products?
- Which association publications will carry advertising, and will there be limitations placed on how much advertising can be sold in each publication?

- Will the association endorse company products and, if so, how will the association's reputation and credibility be protected?
- What limitations, if any, will be placed on giving corporations access to members via selling members' email addresses or by other means?

Aside from addressing these strategic issues, the board should support professional staff in strategy execution. I have seen boards fail in this regard by going to two extremes. Under both extremes, board members demonstrate by their actions a lack of understanding or interest in forging win/win relationships with the association's corporate partners.

On one extreme, some board members seem to have a mindset that the association is doing a favor to any company that wants to engage with it. They ignore the fact that companies are under increasing pressure to maximize their return on investment and in most cases have viable alternatives aside from your association for reaching members. These board members ignore requests from staff to visit and personally thank exhibitors and corporate sponsors at the annual meeting as well as requests for them to attend key meetings with corporate executives.

On the other extreme, some board members who have strong personal relationships with specific companies act as lone rangers. They bypass coordination with their association's professional staff who are charged with nurturing corporate relationship building. In many cases board members make high-pressure demands for corporate dollars that may help the association in the short run. However, in the long run, their actions can result in frayed relationships, diminished staff credibility with their corporate liaisons, and a pull-back in a corporation's long-term financial support.

How can board members help an association build strong corporate partnerships? They should make staff aware of relationships they have with current and potential corporate partners as well as specific contacts they have within such companies. They certainly should feel free to suggest ideas and tactics for engaging with these contacts. They should also notify staff if they become aware of concerns or opportunities for new corporate support that are shared by their contacts.

However, aside from offering such input, board members should let staff take the lead role in crafting and implementing engagement plans with each specific company that are in line with the association's overall corporate relations strategy. To the extent possible, board members should support such plans with their active involvement in corporate meetings scheduled by staff and in showing appreciation to the association's corporate partners whenever possible.

Finally, board members collectively should monitor satisfaction levels as reflected in annual meeting exhibitor surveys, focus groups of corporate liaisons to the association, or other means. Appendix 6.1 includes a set of example questions I have typically asked an association's key corporate partners annually or biannually.

Regardless of the methodology used, the CEO should gather and summarize corporate feedback for presentation to the board at least once a year and communicate action steps staff anticipate taking to address significant concerns and opportunities. Such feedback may result in changes to the overall corporate relations strategy as well as impact other strategic discussions and decision making undertaken by the board.

Identify and Nurture the Best Organizational Partnerships to Add Member Value

Aside from corporate partners, most associations have established formal or informal relationships with other organizations that are teammates in offering value to your members. Many CEOs field numerous requests from various organizations to partner with the association in new or different ways. Such requests range from advocating for specific legislation, to writing guidelines and standards, to joint development and delivery of educational content.

Association boards and the CEO need to determine the types of organizational relationships that are most critical in supporting attainment of the strategic plan and in serving the members. Just as it is impossible for an association to meet every member's desires, it is likewise impossible to respond positively to all requests brought forward by other organizations for collaboration. Many times the answer has to be a polite "no" or the association will risk progress on its key priorities.

CEOs should take the lead role in inventorying current and possible organizational relationships, and categorizing them by priority. Priority 1 relationships should be nurtured, with frequent communications between the board and staff leaders that include strategizing current and future collaboration opportunities. A priority 1 relationship that I was associated with included bi-annual one-day leadership summits with both associations' board officers and senior staff as well as sharing of all board meeting summaries. The CEOs attended each other's annual meetings and were given opportunities to periodically deliver updates to each other's boards.

These and other actions resulted in numerous win/win collaborative initiatives for the two associations, which benefited the members of each.

Priority 2 organizations are important, but receive less attention, with minimal or no systematic communications between the organizations. Requests for collaboration from these organizations, although duly considered, typically receive a higher level of scrutiny given the potential drain on time, money, and other resources that could be better spent on Priority 1 relationships.

Priority 3 represents organizations that need to be on the radar screen, including key competitors. However, they typically are not collaboration partners.

Appendix 6.2 includes a format I have used to categorize organizational relationships, including example protocols for engaging with organizations assigned to each priority. It also presents a template for fleshing out priority 1 relationships. This includes an opportunity to document historical, current, and proposed collaborative initiatives.

Value Your Staff

Aside from members, staff is the most valuable asset associations have. In addition to association profession and functional expertise they bring to the table (e.g., finance, marketing, and technology), each staff person devotes approximately 2,000 hours annually to serving your association and its members.

Although most staff members typically have little experience with the profession or trade served by the association, their careers and livelihoods are tied to the organization's success. Most of them care far more about the association they work for than the professional associations they belong to.

Some board and other member leaders do not understand this mindset. Rather than appreciating and cultivating a strong, mutually respectful partnership with staff, they view themselves as the sole stewards of the association. They devalue what staff members bring to the table, bemoan "staff-driven" associations, and promote an "us versus them" orientation. Taken to an extreme, the member leaders in a few associations might verbally abuse staff or treat them as personal assistants. The results include low employee morale, difficulty in recruiting and retaining high-quality staff, failure to take advantage of staff expertise, decreased member service, and ultimately much lower staff productivity.

To prevent these consequences, board members collectively and individually have a fiduciary duty to consistently build up and partner with their staff. They should look for opportunities to show appreciation verbally and in more tangible ways. Most important, they need to hold each other accountable, simply not tolerating the rogue board member who has a reputation for berating or in other ways devaluing staff.

Aside from their own interactions with staff, the board's fiduciary duty includes supporting, monitoring, and holding the CEO accountable for maintaining a healthy work environment that is aligned with human resources management best practices. The board should:

- Ensure that a human resources audit is undertaken every three to five years by the association's attorney or a reputable human resources consulting firm to identify the extent to which the organization is in compliance with employment law and has adopted best practices in human resource management. The audit should also include verification that the association's compensation and benefits program is in line with the competitive market.
- Ensure the budget includes funds for employee training and development, professional certification, and participation in relevant professional associations.
- Monitor staff turnover levels and the reasons for turnover.
- Pursue recognition as an employer of choice. There are several such programs administered by organizations at the local, state, and national level. I can personally attest to the positive impact such recognition can have in recruiting and retaining the best possible staff. Even if your association is not selected as a winner, the process of applying for recognition can lead to a better understanding of human resources administration changes that should be made. It can also lead to identification of good role model organizations and future benchmarking partners.

One word of caution. Some boards believe their fiduciary duty to staff extends to receiving and acting upon results from employee engagement and opinion surveys or giving credence to the vocalized opinions of a few specific staff members. Such is not the case. Engagement and opinion surveys certainly can be of great value to the CEO, human resources director, and other senior staff in identifying staff concerns and opportunities to create a more healthy work environment. CEOs should be encouraged and commended for undertaking surveys annually or biannually.

However, these same surveys can be used as a club by relatively few staff or board members to build a case for removing an otherwise high-performing CEO, even if the overall survey results are in line with or exceed satisfaction levels found in other organizations. In any organization, there are malcontents, especially if the CEO is attempting to drive a new culture. In other cases, staff may take offense at necessary, but unpopular, expense reductions. Others still are upset when they are held more accountable for their actions than was previously the case. If these malcontents know their responses to employee surveys will be seen by the board, they basically have incentive to sensationalize and in other ways distort their feedback to make the CEO look bad.

With these possibilities in mind, the board should rely on the survey administrator, typically a consultant with a track record of administering numerous employee engagement and opinion surveys, to convey to the board a high-level summary of key results. In other words, the board should not receive detailed responses from individual employees to specific survey questions. The summary should include an indication of how the association compares with similar organizations. If the survey has been administered previously, perhaps a year or two earlier, the summary could also include trends.

The board should dig deeper and perhaps take action to protect its valuable staff asset only if the consultant indicates strong concerns. The same advice holds true relative to the vocalized opinions of staff members. Board members frequently have strong working relationships, extending to friendships, with individual staff. They rely heavily on these individuals to give them the scoop on staff morale and the overall office environment. These staff members' input can be a potential danger for the CEO and the entire organization. Board members must realize that some staff may take advantage of their friendships with them to promote their personal agendas.

Therefore, board members should generally refrain from soliciting such input from individual staff, relying instead on nonbiased data to assess whether or not the CEO is doing his/her job relative to staff management. This includes periodic staff turnover reports, exit interview summaries, and external consultant summaries of employee survey results.

And the Buck Stops With...

The board, the CEO, and the staff are all responsible for win/win relationships. The board should:

- Demonstrate its interest in understanding and building win/win relationships with the association's key stakeholders by devoting time on meeting agendas to the topic;
- Support staff through the budgeting process and personal involvement in forging win/win relationships with external stakeholders;

- Prove by their actions an appreciation and partnership mentality with staff; and
- Hold the CEO accountable for stakeholder satisfaction.

The CEO and his/her staff realistically will be the primary day-to-day stewards of building and nurturing relationships with corporations and other organizations that want to partner with the association. The CEO also needs to be the primary driver of a healthy work environment for the final key stakeholder group—the staff.

Tying It Back to the Members

Certainly members appreciate when their association demonstrates interest in understanding them better and takes into account their input in planning new products, programs, and services. They also appreciate when their association gives them opportunities to engage, to the extent they desire, in the work of the association. Whether in a minimal time commitment role or high-profile, time intensive service on a committee or work team, the result is increased member satisfaction and higher retention levels.

As for corporate and other organizational partners, healthy win/win relationships result in far more resources from them—money, time, and intellectual capital—than associations could otherwise afford. This translates into stronger, healthier associations that are better positioned to bring value to members.

CHAPTER 7

Plan for Future Success

STRATEGIC PLANNING AS A CONCEPT and practice is well established in both the corporate and not-for-profit worlds. If asked, most board and staff representatives of any organization would respond that they understand the value of strategic planning and have a plan of some sort in place. From that point of commonality, there is wide variation in the methodology used to develop strategic plans, the extent to which plans are referenced and reviewed after they are developed, and their ultimate impact on organizational success.

This variation, especially when it deviates from "best practices," serves in many instances to undermine the effectiveness of strategic planning. Following are a few key statistics accumulated from various sources. *The Economist* Intelligence Unit contends that organizations realize just 60 percent of the potential value of their strategies. *Harvard Business Review* has estimated that the average ROI on most strategic planning initiatives is 34 percent or less. And according to Robert S. Kaplan and David P. Norton, originators of the balanced scorecard for organizational performance, 90 percent of organizations fail to successfully implement their strategies.

Research data indicate, not surprisingly, that effective strategic planning and organizational success go hand in hand. A recent survey completed by nearly 1,000 501(c)(3) organization representatives and presented at the 2013 Annual Meeting of the Association for Strategic Planning, asked respondents to self-rate their organization for overall success and the likelihood for continued success in the foreseeable future. Results from this data were used for analysis of planning practices by level of success. Among the key findings:

- Some 93 percent of representatives from high-success organizations indicated strategic planning had at least some effect on organizational success, with 23 percent indicating the impact was critical. Conversely, only 48 percent of representatives from low-success organizations cited strategic planning as affecting their success, with none indicating a critical impact.
- High-success organizations were four times more likely than medium-success organizations to have strategic plans that were perceived as very successfully implemented.

For the Good of the Members

Given the clear linkage between strategic planning and organizational success, why don't all associations have an effective strategic planning process, especially when there are plenty of books and articles detailing appropriate best practices?

Unfortunately a number of barriers stand in the way, several of which can be traced to the unique nature of association governance and the expectations placed on member leaders versus staff. Associations need to break down these barriers if they want to maximize their return on investment relative to organizational planning.

Use Staff Expertise to Drive Plan Development

In the corporate world, most of the onus for plan development rests with the CEO and other staff leaders, with the board appropriately scrutinizing and challenging assumptions and proposed directions before ultimately giving its approval. Some associations do this well with the CEO and staff playing a healthy, collaborative role with the board in this area. However, in some associations, board leaders perceive that it is their duty to drive most of the process associated with plan development, with the CEO and other staff leaders playing a facilitative, supporting role.

Unfortunately, in most cases board members collectively lack the time and possibly the expertise to plan effectively. As a result, what passes for strategic planning is frequently a once-a-year half- or full-day planning retreat. At best, it results in a high-level set of goals and strategies summarized on a few sheets of paper but little in terms of real initiatives that can be subsequently implemented. Yet, board members congratulate each other on accomplishing strategic planning for the year and move on to addressing other aspects of their roles.

What associations need are professionals with the requisite expertise and time to drive the strategic planning process, and similar to the corporate world, those individuals are, or should be, the CEO and her/his staff. Board and other member leaders need to shed themselves of the belief that association employees are not sufficiently attuned to member needs or lack passion and commitment to do what is best for the organization. Nothing could be further from the truth! These are people who purposely chose the association profession and your specific organization. Their very livelihoods depend on your organization's current and future success. Many of them interact directly with your association's members far more frequently than board and other member leaders do, hearing first-hand members' hopes, desires, and expectations associated with your association. Perhaps most important, your staff are better positioned than member leaders to enter the strategic planning process without biases for pet initiatives that may benefit only a small subset of the members.

With staff driving the process, there should be an expectation that best practices are incorporated and adhered to. One critical best practice involves undertaking environmental scanning prior to strategic plan development. As noted by McNerney, Perri, and Reid,[1] high-success nonprofit organizations compared to medium-success organizations are roughly twice as likely to undertake environmental analyses, industry trend reviews, and program analysis/assessment, and are 13 times more likely to conduct interviews, surveys, or focus groups of key stakeholders to better understand their needs and incorporate their input during the strategic planning process. Such environmental scanning needs to be association-specific given that the multifaceted nature of most associations' member segments, organizational relationships, and products, programs, and services makes them far more complicated than most other industries. It requires the direction and oversight of a CEO who is keenly attuned to these nuances and knowledgeable of relevant scanning resources, techniques, and tools.

There certainly remain critical roles for board and other member leaders to play in developing the strategic plan. Staff should individually and collectively engage them at all stages of the planning process, including:

---

1 McNerney D, Perri D, Reid M. "Strategic Planning Practices in High Performing Nonprofit Organizations (501c3)"—research results from national survey sponsored by Association for Strategic Planning (ASP) with University of Arkansas. Presented April 23, 2013, ASP National Conference. Atlanta, GA.

- Collecting and summarizing their input about strengths, weaknesses, opportunities, and threats (SWOT) as well as ideas they have for new strategic initiatives;
- Eliciting the board's reactions and suggested edits to one or more versions of the draft strategic plan; and
- Ultimately securing the board's approval of the plan.

Even these seemingly limited roles can take a substantial chunk of board members' time, especially if done well. And doing them well is a critical fiduciary role that all board members should aspire to.

Create White Space for New Initiatives

In crafting a new strategic plan, many organizations focus only on new goals, strategies, and initiatives that will position them for future success and increased member value. Certainly a future focus is critical. However, strategic planning should also consider what needs to be divested or de-emphasized from the association's portfolio of products, programs, and services (PPS).

Why? Because in most associations, staff and member leaders are already going full throttle with day-to-day operations and administering everything the organization already does. They are not twiddling their thumbs waiting for the next strategic plan with what can be an avalanche of new initiatives to undertake. To make room for new initiatives, and assuming the budget will not accommodate significant staff increases or outside contractors, the association will need to free up staff time. Staff and member leaders need to be given white space to take on what is new.

In the early stages of strategic planning, association leaders should critically review all the association's PPSs, with an eye toward identifying what can be eliminated or de-emphasized. Associations can use several tools for this purpose. Typically, each PPS is considered based on various dimensions, including:

- Member value as validated by member surveys and data regarding actual sales and usage;
- The association's capacity to continue delivering each PPS in line with quality and profitability expectations; and
- The competitive landscape, including perceptions of competitors' ability to match or exceed your members' expectations now and in the future.

Assuming decisions are made to divest or de-emphasize current PPSs, member and staff leaders will be much better positioned to understand the association's capacity to implement its next strategic plan.

Focus on a Few Key Priorities

Strategic planning needs to focus on only a few critical challenges and opportunities. Budgets are typically tight, and most organizations do not have the stomach for divesting or de-emphasizing more than a few PPSs.

Limiting an association's focus is easier said than done! Association boards and their CEOs are continually bombarded by members with ideas for new PPSs. The bombardment intensifies when it comes time to develop the next strategic plan. Many suggestions appear to be excellent, at least on the surface, and it's difficult to say no. As a result, many strategic plans include more initiatives than an organization double its size can reasonably accomplish during the three to five years for plan implementation. Do not be caught in that trap!

In developing your next strategic plan, focus on no more than two or three critical issues that need to be addressed and on no more than five specific new initiatives to undertake in addressing them over the next three to five years. At that point, those involved in the planning process should take time to assess resources, including time, money, and the specific staff departments and committees that will need to be engaged to effectively implement new initiatives. When this exercise is completed, if there are anticipated resources available to undertake more, then consideration can be given to adding more goals, strategies, and initiatives to the strategic plan.

Avoid a Flavor of the Year Mentality

A key difference between corporate and association governance, as discussed earlier, is the stability of board leadership. Outside the association world, candidates for President of the United States, senators, and governors frequently campaign on a platform for change. Candidates for association leadership positions frequently mimic this approach, perceiving a need to make their mark by addressing a specific concern or launching a pet initiative. In many cases, their campaign for office is centered on such a theme. Once elected, the entire strategic plan, or a large portion thereof, becomes focused on achieving the new chair's priority.

Platforms for change are totally appropriate for a U.S. Presidential candidate running for a four-year term of office or a senatorial candidate's six-year term. Such time periods correspond well with the traditional three- to five-year time frame for strategic planning. It provides a large block of time for the articulation and implementation of various initiatives that can truly change the course of the country or a specific organization.

The situation is much different in associations, where the typical term of office for the chair is one or two years. What happens to associations when they experience annual changes in direction driven by the current year's chair? Organizational whiplash! Volunteer and staff time as well as money are diverted from other aspects of the strategic plan to ensuring progress is made on the new priority, which may or may not be valued by the majority of an association's members. After the chair's term of office ends, more often than not the impact continues to be felt. Such chair-dictated initiatives rarely die a quick death and continue to suck time and monetary resources away from other priorities that would be more valued by the vast majority of association members.

In some cases a chair's priority does indeed die a quick death, with serious implications for the association's credibility with other key stakeholders. One American association I worked with had an incoming chair who made clear his strong priority for engaging with comparable international associations. A comprehensive strategy was developed along those lines and aggressively implemented by the CEO, who devoted more than a third of his time—and significant time on the part of his underlings—to engaging with international counterparts and negotiating with them several multifaceted memorandums of understanding.

However, with a change in board leadership the next year, the priority shifted back to a domestic agenda. The international budget was slashed, including most collaboration initiatives already in progress. Can you imagine what the leaders of the international counterpart organizations felt about this change in direction? How do you think they will respond a few years later if new leaders of the organization decide to reverse course again and re-engage internationally? Bottom line, all the international good will that had been cultivated evaporated overnight, and the implications will be long-term.

No matter if a chair's priorities are dropped after one year or linger on indefinitely, the association inevitably progresses in a *zig-zag* fashion toward the attainment of its key goals and objectives, much like the approach our dog Teddy takes on his walks. Meanwhile the association's competitors who take a straight-line approach will get to the destination quicker and may very well steal your members in the process.

With this in mind, the role of the chair in defining organizational priorities should be de-emphasized. Rather than unilaterally setting strategic direction, the chair needs to instead be focused on teaming with board colleagues and the CEO to support implementation of the current strategic plan. This change in mindset can be reinforced by policy and the association's nominating committee, through prohibitions of platforms and themes as part of the campaign process. Once in office, the chair should demonstrate restraint in pushing changes in strategic direction, unless clearly warranted by changes in the association's operating environment.

But what about the argument that this approach takes away a chair's authority and prerogative? After all, attaining the position of chair of an association is a huge accomplishment, typically coming only after years of personal sacrifice, countless hours of volunteering time and energy, and frequently little recognition along the way. All true, but there are many other ways for an association to creatively and appropriately demonstrate its appreciation and recognition of the chair during his/her term in office without affecting the trajectory of the organization's progress on strategic plans that have been collectively developed and vetted by all key stakeholders.

Clarify and Appropriately Assign Accountability for Plan Attainment

In the corporate world the assignment of accountability is typically a nonissue, because the buck almost always stops with the CEO. With associations there is frequently less clarity. The board, committees, work teams, and individual member leaders all typically want to be involved in implementing strategic plans. In the process, I have personally witnessed turf battles between various governance entities, as well as between governance entities and staff, relative to making implementation-related decisions. In other cases, implementation-related activity slips through the cracks, or member leaders assigned accountability for a task fail to meet key deadlines because of competing priorities for their time.

At the end of the strategic plan development process, it is important to articulate clear accountability assignments. A single staff leader and a single member leader should be assigned to most plan initiatives, along with charges to each individual to minimize future confusion and facilitate a smoother implementation process.

Speaking of implementation, this is where the strategic planning process falls short across the spectrum of all industries, not just associations. Too many strategic plans, no matter how impressively documented, remain on the shelf. I have seen firsthand the impact of shelved strategic plans during interactions with countless consulting clients. Recently I facilitated a board retreat during which I asked participants to assess progress the organization had made in implementing its current strategic plan. It became clear that more than half of the board members were unaware that one of the five goals existed. After an initial year of implementation progress, nothing more had been accomplished toward goal attainment during the most recent two years.

Although not specific to associations, it is important for the board and the CEO to address some of the key reasons for ineffective strategic plan implementation, along with recommendations for getting the best strategic plan ROI for the organization.

Link Strategic with Operational Planning

Too often the planning process ends without a clear definition of specific initiatives and milestones to achieve during the time covered by the plan. Without such a definition, goals and strategies typically remain aspirational, with little demonstrated progress in their attainment one to three years down the road.

A sound operational plan creates the necessary bridge from strategy to results. Since much has already been published on operational plan development, there is no need to reinvent the wheel here, other than to convey a simple format I have found useful for this purpose. (See Exhibit 7.1.) Note that the format includes identification of overall board and staff accountability for initiative attainment; details of their specific roles are articulated elsewhere. It also includes specific milestones slated for completion in the first year of plan implementation and draft milestones for subsequent years. This process assumes that prior to the start of each subsequent year the milestones are fine-tuned based on progress, or lack thereof, during the preceding year. To the extent possible, the milestones should conform to the SMART approach. They should be specific, measurable, attainable, relevant, and time-defined.

Drive Accountability and Recognition for Plan Success

It is well known in the human resources management world that what gets recognized and rewarded gets accomplished. Unfortunately, many staff performance management systems and compensation programs lack clear ties between the attainment of strategic plan milestones and individual year-end performance ratings, with accompanying impacts on base salary adjustments or incentive plan payouts.

Accountability within the staff organization starts with the CEO. As discussed in Chapter 5, all CEOs should have their performance formally assessed by the board at least annually based on a predetermined set of performance metrics and competencies. One of the key metrics should

Exhibit 7.1

Organization X 201X–1X Strategic Plan Template

Goal 1: _____.

Strategies with Initiatives Supporting Goal Attainment:

Strategy 1: _____

Initiatives/Accountability	Anticipated Milestones FY 201X	Anticipated Milestones FYs 201X–201X
Undertake _____ Board Lead: _____ Staff Lead: _____	• _____	• _____
Administer _____ Board Lead: _____ Staff Lead: _____	• _____	• _____
Identify _____ Board Lead: _____ Staff Lead: _____	• _____	• _____
[EXAMPLE FOLLOWS]		
Implement protocols and procedures for increasing continual engagement with corporate partners by Organization X volunteers and staff. Board Lead: _____ Committee Chair Staff Lead: _____	• Staff and volunteer roles, including _____ Committee charges, are updated by 9/30/1X and included in the board orientation manual. • FY1X corporate support commitments are obtained from all corporate partners by the end of each corporate partner's budgeting cycle.	• A corporate partner satisfaction survey is administered, with results presented to the board.

• • •

relate to the attainment of strategic plan milestones slated for completion that year. Exhibit 7.2 includes an example of how such a metric has been documented within the context of a set of metrics.

In this particular example, the assumption is that the defined plan milestones are by no means a slam dunk to attain. A less aggressive set of milestones may result in higher threshold, target, and superior performance levels (e.g., 75 percent, 85 percent, and 95 percent). The board may want to adjust the percentages from year to year if it becomes clear that the CEO

Exhibit 7.2

CEO Metrics Planning Form

January 1, 20XX – December 31, 20XX

Performance Metrics	Strategy or Job Description Reference	Measurement Approach	Necessary Conditions/ Resources	Weight	Threshold Performance	Target Performance	Superior Performance
Strategic Plan Attainment	JD: Operations	Year-end assessment by the board's Executive Committee, based on input provided by the CEO and staff.	Excludes consideration of items designated by the Executive Committee as postponed or deleted due to changing conditions. Includes consideration of milestones that were added during the year.	25%	75% of strategic plan milestones identified for completion in FYXX are assessed to be complete.	85% of strategic plan milestones identified for completion in FYXX are assessed to be complete.	95% of strategic plan milestones identified for completion in FYXX are assessed to be complete.
Metric 2							
Metric 3							
Metric 4							

Total Metrics Weight: 100%

• • •

is always meeting or exceeding the superior level, perhaps indicating too little stretch in setting milestones or, conversely, never attaining at least the threshold level despite perceptions that the CEO is high-functioning and doing everything possible to drive plan implementation.

It is also important to note that not all milestones need to be weighted the same. For example, in one association I worked with, the overriding organizational priority one specific year was implementation of a new technology platform. Attainment of that milestone received a weight five times greater than other considerations relative to performance assessment and compensation implications.

As someone who has been subject to a performance metric for most of my years as an association CEO, I can personally attest to how it has helped keep me continually focused on strategic plan implementation. But as important as it is to engage the CEO, in reality most of the true work is accomplished by the CEO's staff. Therefore, it is important to similarly reinforce ties between strategic plan implementation and reward/recognition at all staff organizational levels.

Assuming performance metrics are a part of the annual staff performance planning and assessment process, attainment of strategic plan milestones should be incorporated as a heavily weighted metric. For example, the marketing director could have a metric relating to completion of milestones where he/she has been assigned primary accountability for attainment. This accomplishment, in turn, can impact the size of the individual incentive award each person receives.

This focus on individual/function-specific strategic plan milestones should be balanced with an organization-wide incentive plan that motivates all staff to contribute to the attainment of all strategic plan milestones, regardless of whether accountability for a specific initiative has been assigned to them.

Following is a simplified example of how such a plan can be constructed, which I have effectively used in organizations where I have served as CEO:

	Threshold	Target	Superior
Incentive Plan Award Levels as % of Salary			
Directors	X%	Y%	Z%
Managers	½ X%	½ Y%	½ Z%
Professional Staff	¼ X%	¼ Y%	¼ Z%
Performance Metrics, Weights, and Performance Levels			
Percent completion of plan milestones (50% weight)	75% complete	85% complete	95% complete
Metric 2 (25% weight)	To be defined	To be defined	To be defined
Metric 3 (25% weight)	To be defined	To be defined	To be defined

In this case, half of the incentive award value is tied to how the association performs on the collective bucket of all strategic plan milestones assigned for completion that year—a powerful reinforcement to the value of the plan. Even if a staff member is not personally accountable for a single milestone, he/she is focused on doing whatever it takes to support colleagues who do have accountability. Some organizations have developed creative communication tools, such as a thermometer, to visually demonstrate the rise of completed milestones during the course of the year. This tool can be referenced during staff meetings and made available for viewing on the organization's intranet.

The CEO or HR leader should consider a special celebration when 25 percent, 50 percent, or 75 percent of milestones slotted for completion in a year have been assessed as complete, or when a heavily weighted metric is completed. This could include something as simple as springing for donuts or ice cream on a chosen day.

Switching gears to the governance structure, member leaders who are slotted to play key roles in plan implementation activity often do not see a tie between performance and impact to their continuing roles in organizational leadership. Such member leaders, typically committee chairs and members, should be recognized for progress made on plan milestones by reappointment or progression to higher leadership positions. Those who fail to meet deadlines or in other ways do not contribute as expected to milestone completion should be counseled out of their current positions or, at a minimum, not be rewarded with positions of increasing stature and responsibility.

Make the Plan a Living Document

Strategic plans are most relevant the day the ink dries on the document. Beyond that, changes in the organization's operating environment—both new opportunities and unforeseen threats—can make the entire strategic plan, or a portion thereof, immediately obsolete.

Blind adherence to implementing plans in such instances can have an extremely detrimental impact on the organization's future. I have seen some boards at least temporarily ignore a threat or take a pass on a revenue-generating initiative because monetary resources and staff time are fully committed to implementation of the original strategic plan. In other instances, a new initiative is added to the list without a corresponding reprioritization of what is already slated to be accomplished. Over time, the strategic plan becomes a mile wide and an inch deep, with little accomplished in time to make a big difference in the organization's trajectory. Neither option is in any organization's best interests.

The key to avoiding a stale strategic plan is ensuring that the current plan receives at least some attention systematically throughout the year. It should appear at least quarterly as a recurring item on board meeting action or consent agendas, assuming the board meets at that frequency. There should be more in-depth review by the Executive Committee at other points during the year. This should serve three purposes:

1. Tracking and ensuring progress is being made on the implementation of current strategic plan milestones. McNerney, Perri, and Reid note that high-success nonprofit organizations are three times more likely to undertake such periodic assessment and reporting of strategic plan progress than medium-success organizations.
2. Providing a forum for delaying or deleting initiatives and milestones from the strategic plan based on changes in the operating environment or other reasons.
3. Giving member leaders and staff opportunities to bring forward ideas for new initiatives and milestones in response to emerging concerns and opportunities.

Exhibit 7.3 presents a portion of a template update memo to the board, presumably completed by the CEO, which addresses all three purposes. Exhibit 7.4 provides a template for an accompanying, more detailed report

Exhibit 7.3

Board Memo Template

A total of 25 20XX milestones pertaining to the 20XX–20XX strategic plan were approved by the board in December 201X. Following is the first quarter FY1X summary of performance vis-à-vis the milestones (see accompanying document). This includes:

- An indication of which milestones are complete, on-target, and delayed. If delayed, you will see commentary relative to the reasons for the delay and how we suggest proceeding.
- Requests to add, delete, or modify the milestones based on changes to the operating environment and other recent developments.

Through March 31, 20XX (end of the FY1X first quarter):

- Five milestones have been completed.
- Fifteen milestones remain on target for completion.
- Three milestones are perceived to be delayed.
- Changes or deletions have been suggested for two milestones based on one or more of the following reasons:
  - Committee leadership direction;
  - Changes to external conditions; or
  - New information.

I am requesting that we add the following initiative and milestones to the 20XX–20XX strategic plan:

- Education Goal, Strategy A: As defined in the strategic plan.
  - New Initiative: As proposed.
    - New 20XX Milestone: As proposed.
    - New 20XX Milestone: As proposed.

Rationale for these additions, along with the accompanying budgetary and member/staff time implications are as follows. To make room in the budget and staff workloads for this initiative, I include several recommendations for delaying progress on initiatives that I perceive to be of lower priority or less time sensitive.

• • •

Exhibit 7.4

Association X 20XX–20XX Strategic Plan Implementation Status Update

Education Goal:

As defined in the strategic plan.

Strategies with Initiatives Supporting Goal Attainment Strategy 1:

As defined in the strategic plan.

#	Initiative/ Accountability	Anticipated FYXX Milestones	Projected Completion	Status Update
E1	Undertake an education needs assessment. Board Lead: As assigned Staff Lead: As assigned	• Research is conducted, compiled, and sent to the relevant committees.	4/30/XX	On-target
E2	Update the Annual Meeting format to improve the quality and appeal of meeting content. Board Lead: As assigned Staff Lead: As assigned	• The annual meeting evaluation survey is refined to better capture participants' experiences at other annual meetings and ideas for enhancing our meeting. • A benchmarking report is prepared to 1) summarize common and best practices utilized by relevant societies relative to annual meeting management, and 2) provide recommendations for implementing best practices.	2/15/XX 7/31/XX	Complete Delayed. Target benchmarking partners have been providing their input slower than anticipated. We have moved the projected completion date back a month.
E3	Collaborate with Organization Y on the development of a new online education course addressing ___. Board Lead: As assigned Staff Lead: As assigned	• A memorandum of understanding defining roles, milestones for course development, and financial contributions is negotiated and finalized.	N/A	Deletion proposed. Organization Y has decided it would prefer to develop a course on its own.

• • •

to the board, documenting progress and proposed changes milestone by milestone.

When proposing additions to the strategic plan, assessing budgetary implications can be relatively straightforward. It is much more difficult to project what the implications will be on staff workload and member time. I have heard all too often from both board and staff proponents of a new initiative that it will take "only a few days" to complete, only to subsequently experience a three-fold or more increase in the actual time commitment. Given that staff at most associations are at near or full capacity in terms of workload, with minimal white space to take on something new, it is imperative that overly conservative estimates for staff/member time are considered before approval of a strategic plan addition. Boards should also consider delaying or deleting one or more current plan initiatives to make way for what has been newly proposed.

And the Buck Stops With...

The CEO should be the primary driver of the strategic planning process. This includes:

- Facilitating pre-planning environmental scanning;
- Preparing the draft plan;
- Ensuring timely and effective implementation of initiatives;
- Tracking progress on plan milestones; and
- Systematically fine-tuning strategies, initiatives, and milestones.

Doing it right requires a level of expertise and far more time and energy than the board chair or any other member leader can reasonably give.

However, the CEO needs a very strong supporting cast, not just staff who will be undertaking most of the work but also strong partnerships with the board chair, remaining board members, committee chairs, and other member leaders. These individuals need to support the defined planning process and all of its components. They should collectively put aside their individual preferences and keep in mind that that the strategic plan is all about driving future success of the organization for the good of the industry or profession and, ultimately, the best interests of individual members.

Tying It Back to the Members

An organization or individual chooses to spend money and time on a trade association or society because of value provided. They will renew their commitment by paying their dues only if perceptions of value remain the same or increase.

The best way to ensure your members value your association is to understand what they value based on continual environmental scanning. Association leaders should use this understanding to develop a robust strategic plan that is laser focused on a few key priorities and followed by effective implementation. This process can be difficult for associations because of their tendency to get involved in far too many lines of business with accompanying products, programs, and services. In comparison, their corporate counterparts are typically much more laser focused.

Good strategic planning involves making tough choices among competing options, with a willingness not to undertake some strategies and initiatives for the sake of timely and effective implementation of what is best for the members. With the right strategic plan in place and with staff and member leaders strongly focused on its implementation, your association will be well equipped to take on its competitors, while increasing member loyalty and commitment.

CHAPTER 8

Identify and Manage Risks

Patricia (Pat) Blake, who in 2001 was serving as Executive Director of the Emergency Nurses Association (ENA), had a million thoughts running through her mind the morning of September 11, 2001, as she attended a nursing convention in Washington, DC. It was hard to focus on this convention as she reflected on what lay in store for her the rest of the week. She was scheduled to hop a plane that evening to Orlando, Florida, after which she would embark on a week jam-packed with activity and commitments. Her schedule included the organization's General Assembly, with hundreds of delegates discussing/debating resolutions and bylaw amendments, followed by various committee meetings, social and educational events associated with ENA's annual meeting.

Already hundreds of ENA staff and members were on the ground in Orlando. Staff were overseeing logistical arrangements, while members were participating in meetings or enjoying a day or two of fun before the General Assembly began.

One thought that was not running through Blake's mind was the possibility of two airplanes being flown into the World Trade Center that day, another airplane crashing into the Pentagon, very close to the nursing convention she was attending, and a fourth crashing into a Pennsylvania field. Yet that was the reality Blake faced when she stepped out of the nursing convention and into the chaos that surrounded her. Her evening flight canceled, she scrambled to rent a car, and hit the road early the next day for a long drive to Orlando, contemplating along the way this crisis that not only gripped the entire world but also was about to have a profound impact on ENA's largest annual educational event and revenue generator.

Meanwhile, back in Des Plaines, Illinois, remaining staff at the headquarters office were in near panic mode. Nothing could have prepared them for the situation they faced. With virtually all communication channels temporarily shut down, including cellular service, their boss could not be reached, and there were a boatload of decisions looming. What should members be told about the annual meeting? Would it be cancelled or go forward as scheduled? One way or the other, how should messages be delivered to the thousands of meeting registrants across the country, given staff did not know which of them were already in Orlando, in transit, or still at home? At that time many people did not have access to cellphones or the internet. What should be done to ensure the safety of staff and members already in Orlando, and what should staff be doing, if anything, to continue preparing for the upcoming meetings? Who else besides convention center and hotel staff, audio/visual and other vendors supporting the meeting, and exhibiting companies needed to be consulted? These were just a few of the decisions that had to be addressed quickly and appropriately.

To make a long story short, thanks to fast, clear thinking on the part of ENA's member and staff leaders, a potentially disastrous situation for the organization and its members was averted. The scheduled meetings were cancelled, with members and staff already in Orlando well taken care of by hotel staff until they could make travel arrangements to return home. Members, staff, exhibitors, and other anticipated attendees not already in transit were notified in time to put the brakes on their travel plans. Fortunately, because of prudent negotiation of a comprehensive insurance policy months before, ENA's financial losses were minimized.

What about your association? Are you confident that your member and staff leaders would respond quickly and appropriately to a disaster? Unfortunately, disasters are not isolated occurrences. It is rare that a week goes by without unanticipated world events, acts of nature, contagious diseases, and the actions of deranged individuals, including workplace gun violence.

Disasters have the potential to cripple, if not kill, organizations. Many organizations' leaders, no matter how talented in other regards, are simply not up to the challenge of handling unanticipated events without the benefit of significant forethought and planning. Aside from disasters, associations face numerous additional risks to their short- and long-term existence. Although some of these can be easily mitigated by insurance policies, others cannot.

Risk management is not a topic most people consider as they work their way up the governance or staff structure of an association. The association's future strategic direction and a myriad of critical and unfortunately often noncritical operational issues dominate their thoughts and activities.

More specific to member leaders, very few come from professions or jobs where risk management is front-of-mind, and many lack interest in learning or dealing with it. Based on my own experience as a CEO, risk management topics are typically the first ones shed from jam-packed board meeting agendas. Even if they are given a short time slot, board members rarely demonstrate much of an appetite for discussing them. The implied assumption is that staff has the situation under control.

Unfortunately, that is frequently not the case. Risk management may be one of many things on the minds of some staff leaders. However, in the midst of addressing too many other priorities, it can easily get lost in the shuffle, leading to an overall lack of organizational preparedness. Before the association realizes what is happening, it is too late to do anything. The members, the backbone of the association, ultimately suffer the consequences.

For the Good of the Members

Bad things happen even to the best run organizations, making risk management one of the key fiduciary duties board and staff leaders face.

Director liability, property, event cancellation, and other forms of insurance certainly are important to mitigate damages associated with many challenges posed by the operating environment. However, insurance alone is not enough and is unavailable to cover many of the biggest risks an association faces. Your association, and ultimately the interests of its members, are best served when the board and staff leaders are aware of all the key risks they may face, have strategies in place to mitigate these risks, and continually monitor progress in that regard.

Inventory and Categorize Organizational Risks

If asked, most association board members and staff leaders would struggle to list more than a few risks that the organization faces relative to its future success. Yet the process of identifying risks can be eye-opening and can lead to appropriate attention being given to risk abatement.

Risk awareness should extend beyond the obvious issues that can be covered by purchased insurance. It should include consideration of a balanced scorecard of risks and risk categories. The balanced scorecard concept has been around for more than 20 years. Introduced by Robert S.

Kaplan and David P. Norton in the January/February 1992 issue of *Harvard Business Review*, it has since been embraced by organizations worldwide to manage and improve performance at the individual, departmental, and organizational level. As originally introduced, it includes four perspectives from which to analyze performance:

- Financial;
- Customer;
- Internal business process; and
- Learning and growth.

As helpful as the balanced scorecard concept and methodology can be in addressing performance issues, it also has applications for identifying and managing business risks of all kinds—risks that could jeopardize an association's success if not addressed. In the case of associations, risks under the balanced scorecard concept may be categorized somewhat differently than Kaplan and Norton did. Consider the following revised categories, with example subcategories:

- People: board directors, other member leaders, and employees;
- Financial: membership dues, product/program/service revenue, corporate support, and investment capital and income;
- Goodwill: overall public reputation, stature within the industry or profession, and working relationships with vendors and advocacy partners; and
- Property: buildings, equipment, technology, copyrights, and trademarks.

Following are some, but by no means all, questions association leaders should ask to flesh out specific risks your association may be facing within these categories:

People

- Are board members appropriately protected with liability insurance?
- Is the association appropriately safeguarded from conflicts of interests that may arise among member and staff leaders?
- Is the association at risk in complying with legislative and regulatory dictates relating to individuals (e.g., the need for a whistle-blower policy under Sarbanes-Oxley and guidelines for compensating key employees in compliance with IRS Intermediate Sanctions)?
- Does the association have a solid pipeline of member leaders to fill future key leadership roles?

- Is the association prepared to address sudden, unanticipated vacancies of key member or staff leaders?
- Is the association at risk of losing a significant number of staff due to morale problems or poor human resources programming, including uncompetitive compensation and benefits?

Financial

- Which organizations compete with your association for membership dues and engagement? Consider listing the specific organizations that are most concerning to the association's future health and their relative strengths and weaknesses.
- What educational products, programs, and services compete with what your association offers? Again, consider listing specific competitive offerings that are of greatest concern and their relative strengths and weaknesses.
- To what extent are corporate supporters (e.g., sponsors, exhibitors, advertisers, and affinity partners) meeting their ROI expectations relative to their engagement with your association? Focus on identifying your top five to ten partners in terms of total revenue received.
- Does the association maintain and periodically review a sound investment policy that balances the needs of protecting and growing its short- and long-term financial assets?

Goodwill

- What is your association's reputation with the general public?
- How would you address unforeseen and unwanted media attention related to your association or its members?
- Do the companies and individuals comprising your membership view your association favorably?
- How is your association perceived by high-priority nonmember partners (e.g., academic institutions, corporations, and individuals) relative to educational content development?
- Are you at risk of losing partnerships with key organizational allies in promoting your advocacy agenda?
- If you are a national association, is your partnership with state and local components at risk in effectively serving the members? A similar question can be asked by state and local associations of their relationships with the national organization.

- Is the association at risk of being identified as a spammer, thereby curtailing its ability to broadcast email messages to members?

Property

- Are your building and equipment appropriately covered by insurance?
- Is the technology infrastructure (e.g., association management system, learning management system, and content management system) appropriate to the organization's needs and member expectations? Yes, this is a risk management issue.
- Are data and information provided to the association by its members appropriately secured to mitigate opportunities for hacking and inappropriate use by others?
- Are the association's logo and its usage appropriately protected?
- Are other forms of intellectual property protected by copyright or trademarks?

The initial process of identifying and categorizing risks is typically not as overwhelming as it may seem. Based on my experience, it can be completed within a few months. The process should be initiated at the staff level with an assigned project manager who interacts individually with department leaders, asking questions such as those listed above. When departmental input has been accumulated, the risk inventory should be vetted by department leaders collectively, followed by review by the board or a board committee.

Similar to any inventory, this is not a one-time exercise. At a minimum, a fresh look at organizational risks should be undertaken biannually given the fast pace of operational environmental changes most associations experience. The good news is that with an initial inventory already documented, subsequent inventories will take much less time to develop.

Prioritize Risks and Develop Abatement Strategies

Because the number of organizational risks can be overwhelming, it is critical to identify which ones represent the most significant challenges to the association's future success. These will receive the highest priority for risk abatement activity. Lower priority risks may receive minimal attention other than periodic monitoring within staff departments.

Appendix 8.1 presents sample pages from a risk management matrix generated for an organization with which I consulted. The competitor column may or may not be pertinent depending upon the type of risk. The next two columns give the staff and board opportunities to detail the perceived significance of each risk and risk abatement strategies. There typically will not be a defined strategy for relatively low-risk items.

A scorecard like this should be incorporated in board orientation materials and ideally discussed in its entirety during the first board meeting of each fiscal year.

Make Risk Management a Recurring Board Meeting Agenda Item

Although risk management typically receives little board attention during the course of a given year, the topic is too important for any organization's future to let that happen. At a minimum, staff should prepare a quarterly or semiannual progress report to the board members, updating them on the operating environment and risk abatement activities for the most significant risks.

Even better, allocate time at selected board meetings for presentations by external experts on specific risk management issues. Experts may include the association's insurance broker, attorney, and auditing firm. Representatives from these entities can share valuable perspectives on specific risk management issues and horror stories they have experienced with other clients. This can subsequently lead to productive board discussions and heightened awareness of board and staff leaders' fiduciary duties for risk management.

Digging a Little Deeper

Although there are many risk elements to consider in using the balanced scorecard concept, several deserve specific mention and attention given their importance to virtually all associations. These include crises related to:

Risk Description	Risk Mitigation Strategy
• Lost access to the organization's facility(s) or technology	Business Continuity Plan
• The ability to produce the annual meeting and other key events	Key Event Cancellation Plan
• Unexpected departure of organizational leaders	Leadership Succession Plan
• Unwanted publicity of the organization and its members	Crisis Communication Plan

Following are synopses of each risk mitigation strategy, including its importance and guidelines for plan development.

The Business Continuity Plan

How would you answer the following questions if your association experienced an act of God such as an earthquake, hurricane, or fire that made it impossible for staff to enter and work in your facility for days, weeks, or even months?

1. For your core business, what is the maximum time you believe the organization can be out of commission—hours, days, or weeks?
2. Would your staff know where they should go and what they should do individually and collectively under such a circumstance, and will they have the appropriate commitment to do so?
3. What is the maximum amount of hard-copy and electronic data you are willing to lose—a day's worth, a week's worth, or data accumulated over even a longer period of time?
4. What would be the financial impact of a critical incident that made your organization inoperable for various periods of time?
5. What would be the legal or regulatory impact of a critical incident that kept your association inoperable for various periods of time?

These are just a few of many questions and topics that any organization needs to consider in preparing for a disaster.

Nearly three-quarters of all for-profit companies have a business continuity plan, according to a recent survey conducted by *Disaster Recovery Journal,* an industry publication, and the consulting firm Forrester Research. Government regulations all but require such plans in critical industries like health care, energy, and finance. Shoring up technology is increasingly a big part of such plans, accounting on average for 7 percent of IT annual budgets in the business community, according to this survey.

Based on anecdotal evidence, the prevalence of business continuity plans in other industries, including associations, is far lower. However, disasters do not cherry pick the organizations they affect. A well-thought-out, documented, tested, and thoroughly communicated business continuity plan can serve to:

- Ensure your association is well prepared, in control, thoughtful, and calm in making the recovery process appear seamless to those outside the headquarters facility;
- Ensure that hard copy and electronic data are secure and maintain their integrity, confidentiality, and accessibility;
- Restore core business processes quickly (e.g., within three days);

- Enable staff to remain productive and capable of performing their day-to-day responsibilities; and
- Maintain appropriate communication channels with the association's member leaders, general members, vendors, corporate partners, and other key stakeholders.

Publications, coupled with internet resources, can provide association leaders with a wide array of advice and tools for developing business continuity plans. However, business continuity is one area where spending money for outside expertise should be considered, given how critical it is to do it right. Generally speaking, the process typically starts with a deeper examination of the risk inventory. It includes identification of key business processes, critical data, and critical equipment that need to be preserved, purchased, or quickly recovered at the outset of a disaster. This step is followed by consideration and fleshing out of alternative risk management techniques, including in many cases the identification of an alternative facility(s) where staff can convene or work.

Aside from initial communication of the business continuity plan to the board and staff, it is critically important that the plan be periodically tested. If, alternatively, the plan collects dust on the shelf, it will be essentially worthless when disaster strikes, and key organizational leaders must make quick, critical decisions under high stress conditions. Testing could include consideration of any number of possible events, including:

- Building destroyed or structurally damaged;
- Building structurally fine, but inaccessible;
- Building accessible, but utilities are unavailable;
- Epidemic or pandemic; and
- Workplace violence incident.

The Key Event Cancellation Plan

For many associations the annual meeting is the biggest single determinant of member value and financial success. Although frequently a component of an overall business continuity plan, it deserves separate consideration. What would you do if a terrorist attack or natural disaster affected the city where your annual meeting was scheduled to take place in the near future? Who would you talk to? What information would you gather and use to make decisions? Who would be responsible for making and communicating decisions? How would you handle complaints?

Hopefully all associations with annual and other key meetings have event cancellation insurance, along with well-defined convention center and hotel contracts addressing weather risks, acts of God, and curtailment of transportation. Following are some, but by no means all, additional must-haves in preparing for the worst:

Documentation

At a minimum, staff should have ready access to the following, all ideally backed up offsite and available through the cloud to key staff:

- Emergency contact telephone numbers;
- List of all registered attendees, including exhibitors;
- Travel itineraries of board members, staff, speakers, and other key individuals attending the meeting;
- Facility emergency plans, including emergency contact information and evacuation procedures; and
- Backup facility identification, including a crisis command center, along with technology specifications.

Incident Management Team

This team, typically including key board officers and staff executives, should be identified months before the annual meeting or other key event and would have the following accountabilities if disaster strikes:

- Assess the nature of the crisis, including the presence of attendees already on-site or in-transit.
- Provide overall direction during the crisis, keeping in mind the
  - Preferences and safety of attendees; and
  - Reputation, financial, and other longer-term impacts to the association.

Recovery Team

This team, composed primarily of staff, also should be identified long before the annual meeting or other key event, and would carry out the crisis management plan if necessary. Many organizations define subteams to address specific needs. These could include a communications subteam to interact with the media and keep the website updated and a technology subteam to ensure technology needs are addressed.

Key Contact Strategy

Contact information and communication strategies should be defined for the following in the event of a possible event cancellation:

- Members of the Incident Management and Recovery Teams;
- Emergency services agencies;
- National weather services;

- Host city government authorities;
- Host city convention and visitors center;
- Host city hotels;
- Travel agency/airlines;
- Insurance agent; and
- Professional Convention Management Association resources, assuming numerous associations are impacted by the crisis

Member Communications Strategy

This strategy should be multifaceted, with the website and social media pages serving as the primary vehicles. The advance program and registration packets should prominently direct attendees to the internet in the event of an emergency. The strategy should also include protocols for establishing a call center to field inquiries of registered attendees, again prominently publicized in meeting collateral materials, and perhaps should include a telephone tree to proactively contact selected attendees.

Even with all the above elements in place, there will be unanticipated aspects to a disaster affecting a key event that will call for equally unanticipated actions and decisions. However, there will be a much higher likelihood that the members' and association's short- and long-term best interests will be served if these plans for action are already established.

The Leadership Succession Plan

Unlike many other industries where property, equipment, or technology is the most critical asset an organization has, people are hands down an association's most critical asset. The governance structure and policies typically address what happens when an officer, board member, committee chair, or other leader leaves unexpectedly. However, there is frequently a lack of forethought regarding how best to replace key staff executives when they depart due to death, disability, or better career opportunities. Depending on when such events occur (e.g., a month before the annual meeting for the meetings director or midway through the budget development cycle for the CFO), the impact on an association's operations can be significant.

Succession planning is an ongoing process that many organizations use in conjunction with training and development programs to ensure an adequate pool of future leaders to support attainment of the strategic plan. However, it is also a critical risk management strategy to mitigate the impact of unexpected key leader departures.

If your association has a strong human resources department, succession plans can be developed and maintained internally. Otherwise, it is best to engage external assistance. Regardless of who drives the process, associations need to:

- Identify key positions—at a minimum the CEO, other staff officers, and directors—whose unexpected departures could seriously affect the association's operations;
- Develop separate replacement plans for each key position, including the possibility of both internal candidates and short-term contractual resources who can fill the gap until a permanent replacement is identified; and
- Articulate specific process steps, roles, and responsibilities that will apply once the unexpected vacancy becomes known.

Take for example the CFO position. The human resources director, starting with the job description as a base, should interact with the current CFO, the CFO's supervisor, and ideally the CFO's peers to identify key attributes, competencies, and skills needed to be a successful CFO in your organization. When these have been accumulated, documented, and approved by the CFO's supervisor, possible internal candidates for the CFO position should be identified and screened against these criteria.

In most cases succession candidates will be assessed as having one or more significant deficiencies. These are not necessarily based on capability but on a lack of experience in the CFO role. The human resources director, in close collaboration with the current CFO, can then customize for the chosen candidate(s) a program of external education, internal on-the-job experiences, and mentoring to better prepare the individual for advancement.

If no internal candidate is deemed strong enough to fill the current CFO's role, even for three to six months, the primary succession plan strategy should shift to identifying external resources to fill the gap. For example, the human resources director and current CFO could jointly approach the association's auditing firm or a temporary accountant placement company and undertake conversations relative to an unexpected vacancy, documenting the results for future reference.

The need for succession planning is most critical for the CEO because of the significant role this position plays in the organization. Chaos and panic can ensue if the incumbent departs unexpectedly and the board's officers are unprepared to at least place a temporary leader at the helm within days.

Making rash decisions without appropriate forethought can result in an avalanche of staff turnover and a complete halt in serving the members.

Most board officers and other board members are already fully engaged with their day jobs and the numerous other association governance roles for which they are responsible. The time for planning is before—not when—an unexpected staff leadership vacancy occurs. This includes ensuring the board is aware at any given time, who it would call on internally to serve in an interim CEO capacity or who they would approach to fill such a role from the outside.

The Crisis Communication Plan

No matter how much attention is given to risk identification and risk mitigation, no matter how many specific plans, policies, and protocols are in place, bad things will continue to happen to even the best run organizations. In many cases there will be a corresponding need to undertake damage control with the media, who collectively are focused on sensationalizing what otherwise might be considered mundane. Unfortunately, they all too often search out the bad as opposed to the good.

We have all seen and perhaps empathized with representatives of organizations who are caught off guard by a reporter's seemingly innocent question. Subsequent negative publicity and the need for damage control can extend to months or years. That individual could very well be you in the future! With that in mind, associations should have a comprehensive and continually tested crisis communication plan in place. It will serve to mitigate public relations risk and manage all information dissemination in response to a media reportable event. The plan should include, at a minimum:

- Identification of spokespeople to address specific situations and topical areas;
- The protocol that will be followed when a reportable event occurs;
- Guidelines for interacting with the media;
- Key messages to convey to the media in response to the most likely reportable events; and
- Marketing and communications contact lists.

For example, the protocol to follow when a reportable event occurs should address:

- Identification of the decision maker in determining if an official statement will be prepared and released;

- Accountabilities for formulating and approving statements, determining the most effective and efficient methods for disseminating statements, and ultimately disseminating the statements;
- The process to follow in identifying event-specific spokespeople and prepping them with appropriate talking points; and
- How media coverage will be monitored, reported to association leaders, and responded to if trending in the wrong direction.

Following are example guidelines, slightly modified from a published plan, for interacting with the media. They are fairly generic across all situations:

- Demonstrate organizational concern about people.
- Explain what is being done to remedy the situation.
- Be open and honest. If you do not, someone else will be to the organization's detriment.
- Never respond with "no comment." Instead explain why you cannot answer the question. For example, "We do not have those details confirmed at this time, and we will provide you with an update when we do have an answer to that question."
- Do not guess or speculate. If you do not know the answer, say so and offer to track down the answer.
- Never speak "off the record." The media can use any information released.
- Never give exclusive interviews during a crisis. All members of the media should have the same opportunity to gather information.
- If an injury or death has occurred, do not release the name(s) of the injured/deceased until all next of kin have been notified.
- Do not provide damage estimates, discuss responsibility for an incident, or discuss legal liability in any way.
- Do not discuss illegal activity at any time. If it is assumed, say, "Police are investigating. We are cooperating." Refer all questions to the appropriate law enforcement agency.
- In cases when media request interviews with family members, provide a liaison to family members for the media so that the family can protect their privacy if they choose.
- Avoid side comments that you intend to be humorous but could be misinterpreted.

- Do not accept hypothetical questions. Taken out of context, your remarks can be very damaging.
- Use everyday language, not jargon, when talking to reporters.
- Provide written materials that give reporters background information.[1]

Bottom line, a poor media response to a disaster or other reportable event can do more damage to the organization than the event itself. Conversely, well-orchestrated media interactions can quickly mitigate a potential public relations risk and may actually turn a problem into a wave of good feelings toward the organization on the part of members and the general public.

And the Buck Stops With...

There is clearly dual accountability for ensuring an association's leaders give appropriate consideration to risk management. On the member side, the board chair needs to drive home with board colleagues the importance of this fiduciary duty. This may be challenging given board members' lack of accountability and experience in addressing risk management while performing their day jobs and their inclination to focus attention elsewhere in their board roles.

The chair, in working with the CEO to finalize new board member orientation and board meeting agendas, should ensure that risk management topics are not given short shrift. During subsequent board discussions on such subjects, the chair may need to take a more active facilitative role than usual in stimulating conversations. This includes personally asking invited speakers (e.g., legal, auditing firm, and insurance broker representatives) and staff probing questions to further flesh out business risks and ensure appropriate risk mitigation strategies are undertaken.

On the staff side, the CEO should play a strong leadership role in risk management, including ensuring that risk inventories are periodically undertaken and developing and implementing strategies to mitigate the highest priority risks.

The CEO should delegate responsibility and hold other staff leaders accountable for identifying, monitoring, and mitigating specific risk issues or categories within the balanced scorecard of risk management. Examples include charging the:

- Heads of finance, IT, and facilities with business continuity planning;

---

[1] Adapted and reprinted with permission from Crisis Communications Plan. Copyright Meredith College. Raleigh, NC.

- Meetings function head for event cancellation planning;
- Human resources function head for succession planning; and
- PR/communication function head for crisis communications planning.

Unless such accountabilities are embedded within the performance appraisal process as performance metrics or key job-related responsibilities, they may not be appropriately addressed.

Tying It Back to the Members

Most of the risk management topics addressed in this chapter are specific to associations as entities and their long-term survival. If your association at some point succumbs to a disaster, whether an act of God or man, one could argue that members will simply turn elsewhere to fulfill the desires, needs, and expectations that caused them to join your association in the first place. However, especially if your association is truly focused on the members, finding an economical and valuable elsewhere will be difficult if not impossible, especially another one-stop shop. That is why association risk management is ultimately important to members individually and collectively.

One aspect of risk management that can be visible and important to members is public relations and perceptions, which can cut both ways. If association leaders prepare well for unanticipated reportable events, they can help steer media coverage in directions that paint the profession or trade in a positive light, instilling pride in your members and perhaps even generating new business opportunities for them. Conversely, if caught off guard with no strategy or protocols in place, the impact of negative coverage can be devastating to your members.

SECTION 3

More Association Leadership Dos and Don'ts

CHAPTER 9

Share With and Learn From Your Colleagues

JOHN GRAHAM IV, PRESIDENT AND CEO of the American Society of Association Executives (ASAE), Washington, DC puts it well: "Generally speaking, every problem an association encounters has been experienced and solved previously by one or more other associations. Unlike most other industries, associations are willing, and in many cases eager, to share what they have learned with others in large part because they do not compete. Any association that recognizes these statements to be true, and actively engages in both sharing and learning from others, will be well-positioned to thrive in the future."

Although many associations consider themselves unique, they have a lot in common with other associations and face many similar challenges. The chapters of this book are full of such common challenges relative to governance structure and composition, role definition, CEO/board working relationships, and interactions with external stakeholder organizations. In addition, most associations operate multiple, similar lines of business, including educational courses, meetings, publications, research and practice tools, and advocacy. Nearly all associations serve customers (members) who have wide ranging needs and expectations, and most associations to some extent rely on financial support from corporate partners who have increasing demands for returns on their investments.

Because of these commonalities, chances are there are lessons your association can learn from others who have blazed a trail before you in addressing challenges and problems. Their experiences can save you considerable time and, in many cases, expense and can help ensure that you consider all relevant factors in making crucial decisions.

Putting aside problem-solving, innovation of all kinds is occurring in the association community. For example, associations are taking creative approaches to engage with members and corporate partners, are using technology to increase staff productivity and mine data to better understand members, and are developing new initiatives to leverage association assets in creating new revenue streams.

As Graham indicated, rather than hoarding their secrets to success, associations and their leaders are generally willing to share their knowledge. A professional society of librarians does not compete with one representing purchasing agents. A trade association representing water treatment companies likewise does not compete with an association serving container manufacturers. Their operational issues may be similar, but there is no danger of member poaching.

But the willingness to cooperate goes beyond perceived lack of competition. There is an element of pride in association professionals being recognized as thought leaders. In addition, and perhaps most important, the underlying purpose of most associations is to educate and in other ways support members in advancing their interests and careers. This translates into a mindset of similarly helping peers in other associations and being a resource to them.

My actual experience supports these assertions. I have been amazed at what peer CEOs and other association leaders have been willing to share with me during annual and special interest group meetings of ASAE and its affiliates at the state and local level. Participation rates typically are high in customized benchmarking initiatives I have undertaken to address a wide range of topics and issues.

Aside from my own experiences, consider the experiences of Dean Wilkerson, Executive Director of The American College of Emergency Physicians. "Not a month goes by that I do not benefit by learning from my peers. For example, we recently decided to build a new headquarters office after outgrowing the facility we've been in for more than 30 years. However, no one on staff, including myself, knew how to undertake a commercial building project. I was able to tap into my association CEO network, which resulted in my undertaking eight full-day site visits at associations that had recently built and moved into new facilities. All my peer CEOs willingly shared the processes they undertook, budget information, and lessons learned regarding what went well and what did not, resulting in a series of case studies that I shared with our board and senior management. I cannot say enough about how helpful my peers have been and the extent it has affected planning for our new facility."

For the Good of the Members

Sharing and learning within the association community translates directly into stronger, more competitive organizations that better meet the needs and expectations of current and targeted members.

Support and Prioritize Association Society Involvement

In an era where belt-tightening is, and probably will remain, the norm, it may be tempting for association boards and CEOs to de-emphasize or eliminate funding for their own involvement in association-specific professional development and networking meetings. Do not make this mistake! It is not just lost ROI opportunities associated with formal education such as online and onsite courses and programs delivered by ASAE. More importantly, it is the lost networking opportunities and related learning that come from personal relationships developed with other board members and CEOs.

As a CEO, I targeted attending at least four (typically more) CEO educational/networking events annually that were sponsored by ASAE and the Association Forum of Chicagoland. I directly attribute to these events my establishment and nurturing of solid friendships and working relationships with nearly 100 current and previous association CEOs, many of whom are now contributors to this book.

It is not just CEOs who benefit. Board members who make the commitment to attend similar events where board members of other associations are present find they are not alone in addressing various governance challenges and can learn from each other. The same holds true for staff at all organizational levels.

In their development of annual budgets for their associations, CEOs, along with finance committees and boards that consider and approve these budgets, should make room for the expense and time related to association community involvement. There are few investments an association can make that will result in a better ROI.

Identify and Cultivate Peer Groups

CEOs and other association leaders should engage formally and informally with one or more defined peer groups—individuals who share common opportunities and challenges in leading their organizations. Many such groups already exist within the infrastructures of ASAE and the various state and local societies of association executives, including special interest groups that periodically meet both remotely and in-person. Others have formed organically over time. For example, the Nursing Organizations Alliance includes more than 60 nursing societies, with board members and CEOs interacting throughout the year formally at events and informally on other occasions.

Association CEOs should take the lead in identifying association peer groups already in existence or in establishing groups where they do not exist but are needed. Note that I specifically referred to groups in the plural, because I have found that different groups can serve different purposes. For many issues the most relevant group will be size specific—associations that may represent very different professions or trades than yours but have similar operating budgets or staff sizes. In other instances, the most relevant group will be the specific profession or trade your association represents, similar to the nursing community just mentioned. In still other instances, strategic issues will dictate peer group development and participation. For example, several special interest groups focused on international expansion already exist.

CEOs and their boards should periodically discuss and strategize their personal involvement in these groups. They should target specific events to attend and determine who should attend them. They should also identify needs for benchmarking information and determine how best to obtain it from peer groups. Key lessons learned by those attending peer group meetings and through benchmarking should be readily shared with board members and key staff.

Be Willing to Share as Well as Ask for Help

Learning, whether a result of attending peer group meetings, informal conversations during a cocktail hour, or issue-specific benchmarking initiatives promulgated by an association's staff or an external consultant, should be a two-way street. CEOs should cultivate, and the board should support, a mindset throughout their association of sharing and responding to information requests from noncompetitive associations. Such sharing will certainly increase the likelihood that others will readily share with you when you need advice or benchmarking data. But beyond that, the process of accumulating information and sharing with others can lead to increased self-awareness. Such self-awareness can perhaps help you better leverage what the association is already doing well or, conversely, refocus attention on improvement opportunities that you may have been neglecting.

As for asking for help, some association CEOs and other leaders view doing so as a sign of weakness—admitting a deficit of knowledge that diminishes their credibility. In reality the opposite is true. Do not be bashful! Asking for input and advice is a sign of strength. The best known leadership speakers and authors will readily admit that a key to attaining their status was learning from others. In asking and receiving input from others, any leader will expand his/her credibility and body of expertise. Just ask Dean Wilkerson, who as a result of asking, is now well-positioned as an expert and resource for others who are considering a new building project.

Follow the Benchmarking Code of Conduct

A final key message related to information sharing is the importance of process. The American Productivity and Quality Center, based in Houston, Texas, has defined a Benchmarking Code of Conduct, easily found by an internet search, which outlines best practices. The code addresses such topics as:

- The legality of information sharing;
- How information should be exchanged;
- The need to respect confidentiality;
- The use of data; and
- How best to interact with benchmarking partners.

The suggested protocols have been refined over many years by consultants and experts with long track records of undertaking successful benchmarking initiatives. Association leaders should give credence to these protocols as they both share and seek information with others.

What Your Peers Have Learned From Each Other

Here are two examples from my own experience, both of which had significant impacts on the associations I served.

> *Corporate Support:* Many years ago I was exposed during an ASAE meeting to what was then a relatively new approach for engaging with corporate partners. It involved moving away from single asset sponsorship opportunities to bundled opportunities that resulted in significantly more revenue to associations and typically much higher corporate partner satisfaction levels. After further investigation, including dialogues with peer CEOs who had embraced this approach, we moved forward along a similar path. The results were as predicted, including six-figure annual increases in revenue for the association.

Telecommuting: To attract and retain staff for difficult-to-fill positions, the director of human resources and I wanted to explore the possibility of launching a telecommuting program. We were able to identify an association located in what is generally perceived to be an undesirable city for association professionals to live. However, it had by reputation a long-standing, very successful telecommuting program to attract the staff they needed to operate effectively. Peers from this association not only willingly shared all of their telecommuting policies and forms, but also sent an HR representative to meet with my staff team, answering their questions and addressing their concerns. This led to the quick establishment of our own telecommuting program, which proved to be very popular and successful in staff retention and productivity enhancement.

During the course of writing this book I asked numerous CEOs for additional examples of what they have learned from their peers. Several, like Wilkerson, conveyed that learning has been continuous over their careers, ranging from assistance in developing a specific board policy to advice in undertaking a key strategic initiative. Following are just a few additional examples that I hope will reinforce the message that engagement within the association community can be very beneficial to an association and its members.

Business Excellence Office (BEO): Arlene Pietranton, CEO of the American Speech-Language-Hearing Association (ASHA), was first exposed to the concept of a BEO at a meeting of professional society CEOs. A BEO is a high-profile organizational unit, typically reporting to the CEO, which consolidates or coordinates responsibility for:

- Strategic planning, including vetting ideas for new initiatives as they arise and tracking/reporting progress on plan initiatives;
- Identifying, analyzing, and facilitating development and implementation of recommendations to improve inter- and intradepartmental operational processes; and
- Training and coaching staff on the use of sound project management methodology, at times serving as the project manager for key strategic, large-scale, multidepartment initiatives.

Pietranton subsequently benchmarked with a peer CEO regarding his previous experience launching a BEO. This CEO willingly shared BEO-related documentation, as well as lessons learned from his own experience. ASHA subsequently launched its own BEO, which has since resulted in significant improvements in productivity and operational effectiveness.

Foundation Assessment: Paul Pomerantz, CEO of the American Society of Anesthesiologists (ASA), on beginning his tenure realized his association operated multiple foundations. Paul undertook a benchmarking initiative with his peers relative to foundation organization design and operational practices. This resulted in a data set and accompanying recommendations that were critical in driving board decisions to launch a shared service infrastructure to more effectively support the foundations and provide a framework for improved collaboration.

Currency Exchange: Peter O'Neil, former Executive Director of the American Industrial Hygiene Association (AIHA), Falls Church, Virginia, currently Executive Vice President and CEO of ASIS International, Alexandria, Virginia, shared an example of learning that took place during a casual breakfast conversation before a meeting of association professionals. A CEO colleague had recently returned from his association's annual meeting, which was held outside the United States. Many months before that meeting, his association purchased the relevant international currency when the dollar exchange rate was favorable. This currency was then sold at a profit to attendees on site and used to pay vendor bills. By subsequently mimicking this approach when AIHA had its own annual meeting in Canada, O'Neil estimates his association realized an additional $25,000 to $30,000 to the annual meeting bottom line.

And the Buck Stops With...

The CEO should drive a mindset of learning and sharing throughout the association, reinforcing its importance within the staff performance management system. For example, I have previously assigned specific expectations for peer group identification and leadership/participation in benchmarking initiatives to senior level staff reporting to me.

The CEO should serve as a role model to his/her staff by taking time to attend meetings of association professionals, participating in benchmarking initiatives (e.g., the numerous surveys ASAE and state societies of association executives initiate each year to gather information about association-relevant topics), and informally reaching out to peers for advice relative to specific challenges and opportunities.

The board should support and encourage association community engagement by the CEO and other staff within the context of budget approval. To the extent possible, board members, especially the officers, should team with the CEO to identify and participate in educational/networking meetings with board peers from other associations. Finally, the board should hold the CEO accountable for sharing data and lessons learned from peer organizations to support board decision making.

Tying It Back to the Members

The number-one reason many organizations and individuals join and continue to pay dues to an association is the opportunity to network and learn from their peers. How ironic that some of the associations that support these members appear content to live in a cocoon, uninformed of innovations in operational practices that could benefit them, and spending unnecessary time and money re-inventing the wheel in addressing problems. Engaging within the association community offers one of the best possible ROIs an association can realize for the health of the organization, freeing up organizational resources to better address member needs and desires.

CHAPTER 10

Heed Advice From Your Attorney

BOARD LEADERS AND MEMBERS COME and go, as do CEOs and their staff. The one constant in many associations is your attorney. In some cases, the same attorney serves an association for decades and takes on a role far beyond just providing legal advice. He/she may even gradually become the association's de facto historian. These individuals have seen it all—the good, the bad, and the downright ugly in terms of how the association works and how its leaders have addressed a wide array of strategic and operational issues.

Even in cases where the attorney is relatively new to an association, he/she can bring the perspective of working with boards and senior staff at other associations as well as a valuable legal mindset that may otherwise be missing during key board discussions. Your attorney can share examples of how boards' decisions or an individual board member's actions can cause significant harm to an organization. Attorneys also can share best practices they have gleaned over the years that have proven successful elsewhere.

Of course, attorneys certainly are not infallible, and boards should not blindly follow their advice. There is a reason why an attorney is frequently referred to as legal counsel, not legal dictator or enforcer. Lawyers are indeed advisors, not deciders. Only the board and staff can or should make decisions.

However, many associations, to their detriment, do not take sufficient advantage of the counsel role. They pigeon-hole their attorney into very narrow roles, perhaps because they have concerns about billing rates and expense management. Rather than seek attorney advice before making key decisions, they tend to call attorneys into service only when a catastrophe has occurred or is about to happen. The adage "pay me now or pay me later" can readily apply to an association's relationship with its attorney.

Ideally, your association's attorney should be a valuable strategic partner, providing critical information and perspectives to the association. Thinking of your attorney as part of the team can be liberating for your board and staff.

A good attorney will provide information about what the law calls for but, more important, explain in layman's terms the legal implications of various courses of action. Your association's leaders should be able to understand pros and cons and the legal and practical rationale for different paths forward. If your attorney only regurgitates the law and does not provide an understandable and cogent analysis of practical impacts, you should think about finding another attorney.

For the Good of the Members

I am not an attorney, I have no attorney relatives, and I have my share of grievances with the legal profession. However, based on years of service with many associations, I strongly advocate erring on the side of overusing as opposed to underusing your attorney. I also believe there is value in associations' partnering with an attorney who focuses much or all of his/her practice on the association world. A list of many well-known attorneys within the association community can be found in ASAE's online Buyer's Guide (asaebuyersguide.com).

All good attorneys will keep their clients, in this case the association board, out of trouble relative to laws and regulations that apply to all nonprofit organizations. Common examples include compliance with:

- State incorporation laws;
- Internal Revenue Code, regulations, and the organization's tax exempt status;
- Governance norms derived from Sarbanes-Oxley;
- IRS Form 990 disclosure requirements;
- The Sherman Antitrust Act and other antitrust laws;
- The Federal Trade Commission Act;
- Employment and antidiscrimination laws;
- Copyright and trademark laws; and
- Requirements pertaining to confidentiality, privacy, and cybersecurity.

The best association attorneys provide guidance extending beyond laws and regulations. Board and staff leaders should elicit and strongly consider advice their attorney has to offer on a wide range of topics, including:

- Identifying governance best practices;
- Helping to manage conflicts of interest;
- Alerting the board to risk management issues; and
- Reviewing contracts and assisting with transactions.

Following are some specific nuggets of wisdom shared by a panel of attorneys who devote a significant portion of their practices to serving association clients:

- Paula Goedert, partner in the Chicago office of Barnes & Thornburg, LLP;
- Jeff Glassie, partner in the Washington, DC, office of Whiteford, Taylor & Preston, LLP;
- Jerry Jacobs, partner in the Washington, DC, office of Pillsbury Winthrop Shaw Pittman, LLP, and general counsel of ASAE;
- Jed Mandel, a founding member of Chicago Law Partners, LLC, and general counsel of Association Forum; and
- Jim Wilson, partner in the Washington, DC, office of Webster, Chamberlain & Bean, LLP.

Advice for the Board

Represent the Collective Whole

Many association board members have the mindset they represent a specific constituency. Some were chosen for board service based on geography. Others were chosen based on a specific subset of membership (e.g., manufacturers, wholesalers, or distributors for a trade association). Others still look around the board room, realize there is no one else of the same gender, age range, or other demographic characteristic and decide they are there to represent that segment of the membership.

Jeff Glassie, partner in the Washington, DC, office of Whiteford, Taylor & Preston, LLP, Glassie cautions against any board member's having such a mindset. All board members must represent the organization as a whole. In fact, directors have legal fiduciary duties to the corporation itself, which must be complied with or any director can be at risk of personal legal liability.

What happens when this advice is ignored? The interests of the organization, and the board as a whole, are lost or ignored in favor of individual interests. Service on a board is not akin to being elected to represent a local interest in a legislative body. And thank goodness for that! Congress and many state legislatures represent perfect case studies of entities that are frequently paralyzed by their members' singular focus on the constituency that elected them.

Closer to home, Jed Mandel, a founding member of Chicago Law Partners, LLC, and general counsel of Association Forum, served an association where board members lost sight of who they were there to represent. They took positions, often publicly, designed to play to the interests of a vocal minority of the members. They thought doing so would make them more popular and help them get re-elected. In fact, it led to a divided board that couldn't get anything done and one in which the members lost trust.

Paula Goedert, partner in the Chicago office of Barnes & Thornburg, LLP, cites an example of a board member from a demographic segment of the association trying to amend the association's professional practice standards to the advantage of his segment and the disadvantage of others. The controversy almost ripped the association apart.

Board members need to realize that regardless of how they were selected for a board slot and who they personally identify with, they must represent the interests of the entire organization. It is certainly important for board members to keep in mind various constituency groups within the association's membership and understand their needs and desires. However, any given constituency's interests may not reflect what is best for the association. Jim Wilson, partner in the Washington, DC, office of Webster, Chamberlain & Bean, LLP, says when he facilitates board orientation sessions, the duties of care and loyalty to the organization as a whole are topics one and two on his agenda.

Beware of the Napoleonic Chair

Associations should avoid a person who seeks the chair position of an association to pursue a personal agenda or for self-aggrandizement. Such an individual believes it is his/her right to move the association in any direction he/she wants to, make decisions on a wide array of policy and operational issues, and order the CEO and other staff around.

Glassie recounts a situation in which the chair of a large certification board started acting Napoleonic, issuing directives to the board and staff and imposing her will on policy and other matters in a way that alienated the other directors. These actions also served to encourage the other directors to mimic the chair, taking actions that also could be considered violations of fiduciary duties.

Jerry Jacobs, partner in the Washington, DC, office of Pillsbury Winthrop Shaw Pittman, LLP, and general counsel of ASAE, notes examples of clients whose chair "hit up" suppliers to sponsor travel and other perks during his/her term of office.

Goedert tells the story of a new chair who telephoned her early in his tenure. She could hear the chair pounding his fist on the table, demanding to know what his rights were as the chair, given, he said, "I'm running the joint now." Goedert says, "What I tried to make him realize, not entirely successfully I may add, is he needed to demonstrate a servant model of leadership. His focus needed to be on helping the board undertake its fiduciary duties and advance the association's strategic plan. Rather than wielding overt power, his influence and long-lasting contributions would come from bringing out the best in his colleagues and collaborating effectively with the CEO."

Unfortunately, some associations nurture a Napoleonic mindset by putting the chair on a pedestal, giving the incumbent all the glory and trappings of a head of state. This can include a glamorous inauguration and party, a large stipend, and various prerogatives. In other associations the chair is encouraged to pick a "theme" for his/her year as chair, with a significant amount of organizational resources (i.e., money and time) devoted to its accomplishment.

Associations, and more specifically their leaders, need to realize the chair and other officers work for the board—not the other way around. Putting the chair on a pedestal or allowing a chair to demonstrate such a mindset is dangerous to an association's well-being, and can represent an abdication of authority on the part of other board members.

Although the CEO may attempt to reign in a Napoleonic chair, there is only so much a subordinate can do in this regard. In the case of a board, only board peers can "discipline" each other. The officers and other board members need to step up to the plate, ideally in private but if necessary during a board meeting executive session, to confront and put a stop to actions that place the organization at risk or thwart its progress. This is especially critical if the association is at risk of losing a high-performing CEO and other key staff because of the chair's behaviors.

When a chair creates a difficult situation, the association's attorney can be helpful. For example, Wilson often addresses officer and board member roles, including limits on authority, during board orientation sessions. The attorney, as opposed to the CEO who works for the board or a board peer who wants to maintain a solid working relationship if not friendship with the chair, can better confront inappropriate behavior and frame a diplomatic solution.

In the certification board case mentioned earlier, Glassie, was asked by the board to address concerns pertaining to the "rogue" board chair with a board training session, but before the session could take place, the board forced the chair to resign. How much better it would have been if Glassie had been brought in earlier to address concerns before the situation became a full-blown leadership crisis.

Avoid Lazy Board Syndrome

The parallel to a Napoleonic chair is a lazy board. In this scenario, several board members—or perhaps the board as a whole—abdicate much of their fiduciary responsibilities. Jacobs has encountered this often when the association board has numerous members. Such boards are simply too large to engage in meaningful discussion and decision making. They effectively cede their authority to the chair, the CEO, or smaller groups, such as the executive committee, finance committee, governance committee, and other board entities.

Simply put, board members legally cannot delegate their fiduciary duties and can rely on others (e.g., a consultant, an officer, the CEO, or a committee) only when it is reasonable to do so. The ultimate responsibility and potential liability that come with their fiduciary duties as board members always remains with them.

Regardless of board size, there are frequently individuals who join a board more for the prestige, camaraderie, and perks than a genuine interest in serving and contributing as an organizational leader. These individuals either don't read board agenda materials or wait until the last minute to briefly scan various items on the plane trip to the meeting. They may pay close attention to a few items of personal interest to them, but they spend large portions of board meetings catching up on emails or surfing the internet—all the more easy to do with conference call meetings. Bottom line, they are not fully engaged because they trust their colleagues, and especially the CEO or officer group, to handle the mundane issues related to association oversight.

Don't fall into this trap of being asleep at the wheel! All board members need to keep in mind they are individually as well as collectively responsible for governing (not managing) the association. Directors and officers liability insurance will not protect board members from liability if they are lazy or, in legal parlance, fail to exercise their duty of care.

This especially holds true relative to overseeing the financial health of your association. Goedert shared the example of a client that experienced a tremendous drop in financial reserves to the point the organization was in danger of not meeting its payroll obligations. The board, collectively lazy given a dominating CEO, was unaware of the financial freefall until it was almost too late.

Some level of fiduciary oversight can certainly be delegated. However, all board members, individually and collectively, need to have a comfort level that the organization's best interests are being served. Specific to financial health, this includes ensuring:

- Budgets are reasonable, with actual performance variances appropriately explained and addressed;
- The external auditor has given a clean opinion of the prior year financial results and has a comfort level with the association's accounting policies, procedures, and controls;
- Reserve levels are appropriate to meet unexpected revenue shortfalls or expense overruns; and
- Long-term investment management is in line with the association's articulated investment strategy.

The CEO and board chair collectively need to be on the watch for lazy board members. Such individuals should be coached into a more active role. Absent success in this regard, steps should be taken to minimize leadership roles they might otherwise have, including committee or external liaison roles, until they can be rotated or removed from the board.

Wilson has worked with associations where board members have been asked to resign when it was obvious to their colleagues that they were not engaged, making room for board members who would attend meetings and be productive. Removal proceedings are rare, but requested resignations have happened.

Build Trust With the Members

Mandel has seen association boards go to opposite extremes in communicating to members. Some boards keep their deliberations and decision making too secretive. Key, controversial board decisions are not conveyed and explained to committee members, state component leaders, and other key stakeholders. Over time, even rank-and-file members grow increasingly restless and concerned about being left in the dark regarding the direction their association is taking. An us-versus-them mindset builds to the point that all trust is lost.

This toxic environment ultimately detracts the board from its fiduciary responsibilities. Precious board meeting time is spent addressing contentious council/committee relationships and discussing increasing demands from other members for transparency. In extreme cases, groups of members have crashed board meetings and insisted on being heard. Members have demanded to inspect the association's books and records, which they are entitled to do. The acrimony can have a negative impact on board morale and on the ability to recruit and retain board members.

In other instances, perhaps in response to the condition just described, the pendulum swings too far in the opposite direction. Well-meaning boards become overly open in what they do, ultimately undermining their roles as board members. People who are not board members are not only welcomed but encouraged to attend and participate in board meetings. Jacobs notes examples of associations' inviting former chairs and board members to attend and participate in board meetings. This involvement can result in the old timers' repeatedly reminding the board about how the association has always done things, which can detract from taking necessary new directions in response to changes in the operating environment.

In other situations, details of board deliberations, including the votes of individual board members on every decision, are conveyed to the entire membership. The result can be a divide-and-conquer approach to challenging the cohesiveness of the board. It can undermine the board members' obligations to keep board discussions confidential and to support the decisions of the board, even if they did not originally vote in favor of them.

Too much openness can stifle the type of candid conversations and tough decision making boards frequently need to have, especially for board members who are insecure about their reputations with segments of the membership or are posturing for re-election or higher office. It is hard to put the genie back into the bottle once a board shares too much information or gives nonmembers too large of a role in making decisions that should be made at the board level.

The key to avoiding either extreme is building trust and maintaining open lines of communication. A board needs to find the right balance between too much and too little interaction with other association stakeholders. Board members, to the extent possible, need to be approachable and available to interact and listen to the members. Highlights of board meetings should be published on the website and in the association's magazine. Ideally, the board will seek member input before making controversial decisions and will share the rationale for these decisions once they are made. Bottom line, if leaders and general members feel valued and respected by the board, trust levels will be high and the board can function without distractions.

If the association's culture still dictates open meetings are a must, Wilson counsels that at least a portion of such meetings be closed (i.e., executive sessions) for sensitive topics or for discussion of attorney-client privileged communications. Attorneys cannot give privileged advice when guests are present during board meetings.

Truly Manage Conflicts of Interest

Nonprofit corporation laws and court decisions require associations to maintain a climate of bias-free decision making for the benefit of the association's constituents. How is this possible when the vast majority of association boards have members who have business or personal interests and relationships that occasionally could influence their association decision making?

Having conflicts of interest (COI) is not inherently wrong or illegal. But the board needs to know about such interests and take them into account when a particular interest or transaction is being addressed by the board.

Some board members are not astute enough to recognize what constitutes a conflict. Other board members at times forget or choose to ignore the impact of their personal conflicts.

What happens when conflicts are not managed appropriately? Many associations have had bad publicity because of board conflicts. Press coverage may have led to assumptions that associations were favoring commercial interests over science or the public good.

Mandel shares the example of an association that lost control of an important new business venture because a board member, who had a self-interest in that venture, was allowed to participate in all the board's discussions and decision making concerning the business venture. In this particular situation, the board member ended up owning the program that the board developed and paid for.

COI should be a key topic of board orientation, including examples such as the one above to drive home the impact of ignoring them. Many association attorneys recommend associations distribute COI forms each year to their board and committee members, asking them to disclose other interests that could become conflicts during their service on the governance entity. COI should also constitute a standing agenda item at the beginning of each board meeting to remind board members of their duty of loyalty and corresponding obligation to disclose COIs as they pertain to specific discussion topics. Directors should not be embarrassed about conflicts, but they do need to be encouraged to disclose them and recuse themselves appropriately.

It is not just during board meetings that COIs arise. They can occur at any time during a board member's tenure. Board members need to be vigilant not only relative to their own conflicts but in calling out COIs of their colleagues.

Protect the Piggy Bank

Many associations are blessed with solid financial reserves, unlike some cause-based and other nonprofit organizations. Unfortunately, some of these associations' boards demonstrate a cavalier approach to the finances. They take risks and embark on grand schemes that go well beyond the organization's core competencies and what individual board members would undertake with their own money.

For example, one of Goedert's clients established, without her being informed, a consulting line of business which directly competed with supplier members. As a result, the supplier members stopped sponsoring the association's events. They also discontinued exhibiting at the association's annual convention and advertising in its publications. Ultimately this new business venture caused the association's financial reserves to dwindle instead of increase.

Boards need to hold themselves to the "prudent person" standard, which includes erring on the side of taking conservative stances. An association's reserves are not play money. I don't mean to imply that boards should avoid new ventures and business opportunities. But such investments should be based on solid, well-thought-out business plans rather than whims or unresearched suggestions made during the course of board discussions. As directors of the association, board members need to take whatever time is needed to make decisions relative to the piggy bank, decisions that can be defended as reasonable under the circumstances.

Wilson counsels his clients to actively seek advice from the association's external financial advisors in assessing the impact of large expenditures and expected returns on reserves. Short- and long-term financial planning for the association as a whole should also be addressed regularly to protect the future of the organization.

Don't Get Too Personal with the Staff

In Chapter 6, I discussed the danger associated with board members' getting too chummy with staff. Too close relations with individual staff can result in these staff having undue influence on board decision making, promoting their personal agendas, and in some cases, subverting the CEO.

Aside from these dangers, Goedert has experienced board members who have found themselves in trouble for what they perceived to be innocent gestures of goodwill and friendship. They tend to forget what a politically correct world we live in. As a CEO, I personally had to address the very difficult challenge of a staff member who perceived a board member made a pass at him. Although litigation was ultimately avoided, it caused considerable hand-wringing within the board, led to a censure of the board member, and resulted in appropriate expressions of remorse to the staff member by the offending board member.

Board members simply cannot let their guard down, especially at social functions surrounding board meetings, where alcohol consumption can frequently lead to problems. They need to realize the bar is set very high in their interactions with staff. Staff expect to be treated as professionals and respected as individuals. Telling jokes in the presence of staff, commenting on personal appearance, putting an arm around a staff member, giving someone a pat on the back (or worse, the rear), and in other ways acting too casually can spell trouble.

Glassie emphasizes that sexual harassment and antidiscrimination laws apply to impermissible conduct affecting staff, whether the perpetrator is a senior employee or a volunteer officer or director. Wilson notes there is actually a case on the books in which a court found the defendant association responsible for an employee's sexual harassment claim based on inappropriate actions of a volunteer board member when visiting the association's headquarters.

Know Who Can Speak for the Board

On occasion individual board members are approached by the media, representatives from affiliated organizations, and other individuals about the board's position on specific issues. It may be tempting to personally oblige such a request and perhaps garner a little limelight in the process. However, Mandel has experienced situations where a board member has taken liberties to convey a position that either has not yet been discussed by the board or inaccurately portrays the board's position on an issue.

Glassie routinely cautions directors that their statements can be legally attributed to the association. Politically incorrect comments can cause trouble, and disparaging statements can result in defamation claims against the individual directors and the association.

Jacobs notes the watershed U.S. Supreme Court decision in the 1982 Hydrolevel case. An association's committee member teamed with a low-level association staff member to issue a negative interpretation of the association's standards. This action ultimately condemned a one-product company to bankruptcy. The association was held financially responsible even though its board didn't approve the interpretation, didn't know about it, and certainly didn't benefit from it. In effect, the Court imposed "strict liability" on the association.

Association board chairs and CEOs need to continually reinforce the importance of deferring requests regarding the board's posture on specific issues to the appropriate spokesperson. Those who are authorized to speak for the association should be given scripts or talking points for use in responding to sensitive issues and decisions.

Refrain From Micromanaging Committees

In Chapter 2, I addressed the temptation some association boards have to insert themselves in operational issues by micromanaging staff. Mandel cautions that the micromanagement tendency can equally apply to committee work. He has experienced a number of situations where a board or individual board members essentially take control of a committee or stifle its ability to fulfill its role, which is to address in detail a particular assigned issue or program and make recommendations to the board.

A board certainly needs to provide clear direction, in the form of charges, to committees that address expected accomplishments. Rogue committees should be reined in when they act outside their scope. However, to the extent possible, committees should be given latitude to work, taking advantage of committee members' interests and expertise and giving them opportunities to demonstrate leadership. After all, committees are a primary testing ground and pipeline for future board members.

Don't Misuse Your Organizational Title

Every association should have a governance policy addressing the extent to which a board director can refer to and use the director title outside the bounds of their board service. Goedert and I unfortunately have the shared experience of a board member who took advantage of the director title to advance her career, referring to the title in promoting a book and speaking engagements. Predictably, this misuse was offensive to many of the association members, especially individuals who were professional competitors of the director.

Examples of title misuse cannot be ignored, or the board as a whole will be perceived negatively as a breeding ground for personal self-interest. In the specific case just mentioned, the board took appropriate action, first with coaching on appropriate title use from the chair and an outside governance consultant, followed ultimately with removal of the director from the board when the behaviors continued.

Appreciate Who Your Attorney's Client Is

Board members should take some comfort in the fact that the attorney(s) engaged by the association is, ultimately, the association's counsel. For day-to-day encounters, the attorney will typically work with and through the association's CEO or other senior staff. But under the law, the board is the highest governing authority in the association. The attorney ultimately reports to the board, especially in situations in which the board and the CEO are at odds or "adverse," the prime example being when the board or a committee of the board is engaging, or disengaging, the CEO.

Jacobs notes the occasional situation in which the board, perceiving it must have independent counsel, will actually engage separate and additional legal counsel to advise the board. That should be wholly unnecessary. The chair, or a group of board members, ought to first meet with the attorney, confirming he or she works for the association as the client and, when there is a potential conflict between the board and the CEO, the attorney is expected to be "on the side" of the board.

Beware of the Domineering Attorney

At times an association's attorney falls into the habit, often engendered by a long-term relationship with the association, of reversing roles with the client, deciding things that should be decided instead by the board or the CEO. An attorney best serves the association, as well as its board and CEO, not by recommending "yes" or "no" but by offering a range of decision alternatives and providing the best assessment of the relative legal advantages or risks of each. The attorney's role is not to approve or veto decisions from an association business perspective.

Advice for CEOs

Lead From Behind Your Board

Napoleonic leadership is not a danger associated with just board chairs. Goedert has witnessed a number of CEOs who begin their tenure with a "bull in the china shop" mentality. This most often happens when such individuals have minimal experience working in an association environment.

In other industries, the strong CEO model works well and is expected. Their board members typically want to keep a low profile, prefer their CEO to be the primary driver of the organization's strategic direction, and leave public relations and advocacy in his/her capable hands.

Such a strong CEO role typically works in the association world only when the organization is in crisis mode. In most other cases, a too-strong new CEO will likely receive a rude awakening.

Most association boards are composed of individuals who are passionate about their industry/profession and the association that serves it. They have spent years working their way up the volunteer leadership structure without compensation and through sacrificing other life priorities. When they reach the pinnacle of society leadership, serving on the board and ultimately in officer positions, it is understandable they don't want to be dominated and under the thumb of the CEO. Instead, they want and deserve a partnership that is characterized by mutual respect and considers their input in making key decisions affecting the association's future.

The best association CEOs recognize this dynamic and instinctively lead from behind. This style of leadership involves making the chair and other board members look good, giving them credit for ideas and decisions that turn out well and deflecting blame when results do not meet expectations. Adopting this mindset not only bodes well for CEO tenure but also ultimately can give the CEO more influence than he/she would otherwise have. When the chair and other board members know the CEO has their backs and best interests in mind, trust will increase, and the CEO's influence with these individuals will typically soar.

Pay Me Now or Pay Me Later!

Good attorneys don't come cheap. Many association CEOs, along with their boards, blanch at the hourly billing rates and the fees they incur each year for legal services. As a result, many CEOs purposely shut out or at best severely minimize interactions with the association's attorney. They perceive they have enough common sense and experience to go it alone in addressing most issues associated with running an organization.

But the real issue isn't cost; it's value. CEOs also must weigh the benefits of not incurring the larger costs, measured in both dollars and unnecessary distractions. Such costs can be avoided by consulting with your attorney up front.

Unfortunately CEOs don't know what they don't know. Consider what Goedert experienced with one of her clients. An association CEO urged the board to send a letter to members telling them not to do business with a specific vendor. The CEO was unaware this action could be characterized as a "group boycott" and a violation of antitrust laws. He found that out when the chair was arrested on grounds of criminal antitrust conspiracy. When Goedert asked why he had not shown her the letter first, the CEO's response was, "You would have charged me to read the letter." That would have been money well-spent!

One of Mandel's clients adopted a policy that the attorney would review only contracts in excess of a particular amount. This association viewed the importance and legal significance of a contract by the amount of money changing hands. It ended up entering into a contract for which little or no money was at stake but in which it allowed another party to use the association's name and logo. But the contract, which was not reviewed by Mandel, did not properly protect or control how the other party used the name and logo. As it turned out, a contract of little dollar value resulted in a huge hit to the association's reputation, given the way the other party used the association's name and logo.

Glassie noted a situation where an association didn't think through termination of a contract and didn't consult with their attorney until the decision to terminate had already been made. There were not legally sufficient grounds for termination, which caused the association to settle the dispute by payment of tens of thousands of dollars to the vendor, which could have been avoided if the association had sought proper legal advice.

Undoing the damage caused when attorneys are not consulted before making business decisions can cost two, three, or more times than the legal fees and other expenses that would have been incurred by seeking legal advice up front.

Mandel advocates that CEOs consult with the association's attorney on even seemingly routine matters. The CEO and the board should have a relationship with the attorney where they know he/she will not look to get involved when legal expertise is not needed and will not "over-lawyer" when simple, straight forward advice is all that is required. The attorney, whether in-house or outside, should act in the role of general counsel and be routinely kept in the know about what the association is doing and be routinely consulted.

That is why Wilson advocates for the attorney to attend board meetings regularly. On countless occasions he has heard something unexpected at a board meeting and leaned over to the CEO to provide advice that later turned out to be critical. If he had not attended the meeting, nobody would have known there was a legal issue to be considered. Attendance also gives Wilson a high level awareness of the association's main activities and issues, which is critical to delivering the best legal advice on individual issues. He also has found his attendance helps board members get to know and feel comfortable interacting with the attorney and vice versa.

Finally in terms of attorney fees, there are alternatives to straight hourly rates, which indeed have the tendency to suppress regular calls to the attorney. Jacobs notes many law firms will agree to handle routine and expected representation—calls and emails, contract review, meeting attendance, and the like—on a monthly retainer rather than on an hourly fee basis. While the law firm will still be aiming to achieve its targeted revenue from client counseling and advocacy, the association will have fixed expenses for most legal representation, which may be better for budgeting as well as for encouraging regular use of the attorney.

Understand the Importance of Timing

Like it or not, most association boards are highly political, with shifting coalitions and leadership styles that one year can play to a CEO's advantage and the next year may result in him/her being in the hot seat.

Mandel counsels CEOs to be clearly attuned to these shifting sands. They should certainly stay above the political fray and avoid taking sides among board members. They also need to be mindful of when the timing is right or wrong to advocate for something that may be viewed as controversial or self-serving.

For example, a CEO needs to be careful about asking for a significant compensation adjustment or a new contract. The timing is key. Rather than make "nickel and dime" requests each year, save up for a larger request in a year when the alignment of board leadership and composition is conducive to a positive response.

And the Buck Stops With...

The CEO and every association board director are responsible to protect the association from risk or decision making that may be detrimental to its success. An association's officer group, and especially the chair, should be attuned to the need for appropriately engaging with the attorney. At a minimum, Glassie recommends an annual check-in to catch up on routine issues and focus on potential issues that might not otherwise be noticed until it is too late. After one such meeting with a client, he uncovered a list of 20 problem issues and identified corrective actions to take. This included a need to secure an insurance policy to replace one that was not adequate. In this way, the organization was able to proactively address issues before they became problems.

In some associations the chair and attorney schedule monthly or bimonthly check-ins to discuss the issues addressed in this chapter, including specific items of concern.

Beyond the formality of scheduled interactions, the chair and attorney will ideally nurture the type of relationship, starting in the chair-elect year if not before, whereby both individuals feel comfortable picking up the phone at any time when an issue related to board duty needs to be addressed. At least once during the chair's tenure, he/she should ask the attorney if the CEO and other key staff appear to be engaging with the attorney on the "right" issues at the "right" time. If the comfort level and working relationships are strong, the legal risks are likely to be minimized.

Aside from the chair, each director should have an open invitation to contact the association's attorney if a question arises relative to the individual's fiduciary role or if the director has a potential legal concern that he/she perceives is not being appropriately addressed by the board officers.

The CEO typically has a longer-term personal relationship with the association's attorney than most board members. This relationship should be collaborative as opposed to adversarial. The attorney ultimately serves the association and, therefore, the board as the association's highest governing authority. However, CEOs should take advantage of the counsel role early-on when considering new directions, new contractual arrangements, changes to the employer-employee relationship, and in other situations where there is not a clear precedent for handling a situation—keeping in mind the adage of "pay me now or pay me later."

Tying It Back to the Members

Examples presented in this chapter speak to detrimental financial, reputation, and other negative impacts various associations have faced when their leaders undertake risky actions or behaviors. In many cases, leaders are completely unaware of what the risks are. Although advice provided by association attorneys should not be followed blindly, legal advice can be critical in negotiations and decision making that serve the best interests of the association and ultimately its members.

CHAPTER 11

Consider Food for Thought From Experienced CEOs

I HAVE SURVEYED MANY CURRENT AND former association CEOs regarding what they believe association leaders should start doing, stop doing, and do better in serving an association and its members. Much of what they conveyed supports key themes presented in previous chapters. However, in several instances, they addressed topics that either have not been covered previously or do not warrant an entire chapter to discuss.

Some advice is directed to the board as a whole, some to the board chair, and some to the CEO. Taken as a whole, this guidance represents several hundred years of accumulated wisdom from leaders who have worked to effectively serve their associations' members.

How to Be an Effective Board Member

Previous chapters have detailed a number of recommendations for board members to consider in effectively serving their association. Following are a few additional tips to consider.

Be Your Association's Evangelists

From Liz Lucas, MBA, CAE, executive director & CEO of Soroptimist International of the Americas, Philadelphia, Pennsylvania: "All board members should be enthusiastic and passionate about the organization, avoiding negativity and always painting the organization and its board in a positive light when interacting with others outside of the board. The CEO can play a key role in this process by giving board members positive messaging about the organization to use and coaching on how best to convey messages."

Focus on the Five Ms

From Scott Herceg, CAE, executive officer, Home Builders Association of Northern Michigan, Petoskey, Michigan: "The five Ms represent a solid framework for board members to consider in undertaking their fiduciary roles and focusing on serving the members:

- Mission: What is the association's mission or reason for existence? Are the board members being true to the mission that they have charged themselves with? Does the mission statement accurately reflect the actual mission of the organization? Are the activities, programs, and advocacy efforts following the mission of the organization? Are the members actively engaged with the mission?
- Money: Is the association being a good steward of the monies it receives from members and donors alike? Is the organization operating in a fiscally responsible manner both in the immediate sense and in planning for the sustainability of the organization in the future?
- Membership: Does the organization strive to grow its current membership base and show a commitment to retaining those members who are already enrolled? Is the organization listening and actively trying to engage its members by providing quality programing that is of value to both current and potential members?
- Manpower: Does the organization have the right people (volunteers and staff) in the right positions, doing the right work for the right reasons and for the right organizational goals?
- Marketing: What is the message of the organization? Does the organization effectively convey its message to its current members, future members, the general public, and others? Is the message being conveyed one with professionalism and relevancy? Does the message accurately represent the mission of the organization?"

How to Be an Effective Board Chair

Board chairs play a critical role in promoting governance excellence in associations. The following advice is specific to this leadership position.

Build on Positional Leadership to Be a Truly Great Leader

From Christopher E. Laxton, CAE, executive director, AMDA—The Society for Post-Acute and Long-Term Care Medicine, Columbia, Maryland: "The foundation of leadership is self-leadership. How would you answer this question: Why should anyone be led by you? The *positional* authority you hold is the starting point of your leadership journey. It is not the destination, and it is by no means the proof that you are a leader. Association board chairs would do well to always remember that leadership is earned, and must be re-earned every day.

How might you do this? First, lead the *consensus* of the board; don't impose your own views and lead by fiat. Make sure that all voices are heard and the culture of the board is safe, respectful, and collegial. Second, make sure you build and maintain a true partnership with the chief staff executive. He or she knows more about how your association functions on a day-to-day basis than you ever will or can. This makes the executive your most important customer. And third, remember self-leadership applies to the board as a whole as well. The board must embrace how to be the best board it can be. And you alone are in the position to lead them to take on this responsibility. Don't let the opportunity pass to make your board the true strategic asset it can, and should, be. After all, it may well be the opportunity of a lifetime."

Focus on the Strategic Plan

From John Barnes, former CEO of the American Physical Therapy Association and current president of Barnes Association Consultants, Alexandria, Virginia: "Make the association's strategic plan the focal point of your efforts as board chair. It will not only ensure you are working on the most important issues facing your association but will allow you to say 'no' when members and staff try to pull you away from the most important issues facing your association. Just remind members and staff that the strategic plan is your highest priority and it will help them to not pull you into other things not as critical."

Combat the "Are We a Member-Driven or Staff-Driven Association?" Argument

Also from John Barnes: "*Member-driven* versus *staff-driven* is a false dynamic. A better and more productive framework for discussions about roles and responsibilities is *member-led* and *staff-implemented.* Member-led means the board is making important decisions for the association at the appropriate level (e.g., approving the strategic plan, making decisions about the direction of your government affairs advocacy, and approving the annual budget). Staff-implemented means staff implement the critical decisions made by the members and manage the association. Move the conversation about the member-staff roles from one of *versus* to one of *and.*"

Engage All Board Members in Discussions

From Chris McEntee, MHA, FASAE, executive director, American Geophysical Union, Washington, DC: "It is important to engage all board members in actively participating in board discussions, to focus discussions on the issues that matter most, and to operate through consensus decision making (i.e., all opinions are shared and valued before a decision is made). The board chair has a great responsibility to ensure alternate views are solicited and encouraged, to ensure no one board member dominates a discussion, and to call on board members who tend to be quieter in group discussions. Your demonstrated skills as a discussion facilitator will go a long way toward keeping discussions in the board room, rather than in the hallways and outside the board room."

Challenge Erroneous Statements Made by Board Colleagues

From Paul Markowski, CAE, executive vice president & CEO, CHEST, Glenview, Illinois: "The board chair *has* to be a leader, which means you will not be able to please everyone. You need to work with the CEO to do the right thing. Allowing a few malcontents to make erroneous statements in board meetings or executive sessions and not challenging the validity of those statements can lead to new perceptions which, even if false, eventually become more of a reality to the board and possibly other members. This false reality can be detrimental to the association and its members."

Lead Your Colleagues Toward a Generative Mindset

From Pierre Désy, MPH, CAE, executive director, International Association of Oral and Maxillofacial Surgeons, Rolling Meadows, Illinois: "According to Chait, Ryan, and Taylor in their book *Governance as Leadership,* there are three modes of governance: Fiduciary (board's role: sentinel), strategic (strategist), and generative (sense maker). Few boards operate at the generative level. Boards that do so engage in less formal and instead more participative work. They collaborate with management to discern problems, explore root causes, values, opportunities, and new ideas to guide strategy and improve competitive position. At the generative level, boards provide technical expertise and act as a consulting firm to bring new perspectives on current challenges, tap into intuitions, and encourage robust discourse.

What can board chairs do to encourage generative leadership? Build more time during board meetings to reflect, invite relevant and thought-provoking speakers, and create more 'So, now what?' moments for the board. Ask questions such as, 'What should we worry about?' 'What is good for our mission?' 'Where is our strategic plan leading us?' As the chair, you can lead your colleagues in practicing generative thinking, enriching the board's performance in serving the association and its members."

How to Be an Effective CEO in Supporting Your Board

Building a Strong Partnership With Your Board

CEOs will be successful only if they cultivate and nurture strong relationships with their boards. The process should start before the CEO agrees to take the job.

Do Your Homework on the Board Culture Before You Accept a CEO Position

From John Thorner, JD, CAE, former executive director of several international associations: "Before you accept a position, make the best effort possible to understand the prospective organization's culture and whether or not you are in sync with it. One of the key elements is understanding what board members want from the CEO and the staff he or she will be directing. Does the board want a servant to carry out board directives without question? Or does the board want, at the other extreme, a strong leader who acts first and informs the board only when an action is completed?

In assessing the culture, you need to look at the current board and officers to determine whether there is unanimity or whether there is a split opinion. You also should look down the road to determine whether the current culture is likely to stay in place for the near future given future board and officer elections.

Once you have assessed the culture, you should resist the temptation to believe you can change that culture. An individual can attempt to initiate a cultural change, but the group has to want to change its own culture. Usually this occurs only when the leaders recognize the organization is facing a financial or membership crisis. And even then, the organization will not be able to change its culture to deal with this crisis unless it has in place a set of strong current and future volunteer leaders who are going to lead that culture change over the next several years."

Really Get to Know Your Board Members

From Denny McGuirk, president and CEO, SEMI, San Jose, California: "There are always issues that arise when interacting with a board. Many of these are due to the uniqueness of each board member—their backgrounds, personalities, and purposes for serving on the board. The CEO needs to be aware of and sensitive to differences and should make adjustments to recognize them. Get to know board members personally and professionally and establish your credibility by showing them you are willing to listen and to learn. Meet with them in person, in their environments and get to know and understand their vision for the industry as well as the association."

Engage With Each Individual Board Member

From Linda Groah, MSN, RN, CNOR, NEA-BC, FAAN, Executive Director/ CEO, Association of periOperative Registered Nurses, Denver, Colorado: "Communicate with all board members on a one-to-one conference call a minimum of two times per year, giving them the opportunity to be heard as individuals and to ask questions they may be too shy to ask in the full board meeting. Such calls create an avenue to get to know board members more intimately than board meetings allow."

Focus on Building Trust

From Lynne Thomas Gordon, MBA, CEO, American Health Information Management Association, Chicago, Illinois: "Partnerships between the board and their CEO must be built on trust. Several years ago, Stephen M.R. Covey, author of the *New York Times* bestseller *The Speed of Trust,* spoke at our annual convention. He talked about the four traits necessary to build and maintain trust: intent, integrity, experience, and accountability. I have these traits written on my whiteboard at work so they are always front and center. Covey says, and I truly believe, 'Trust is equal parts character and competence.' With trust, you and your board can move mountains with agility and ease, since it is one of the most powerful forms of motivation and inspiration."

Bridge the Gap Between Trust and Control

From Mark Engle, DM, FASAE, CAE principal, Association Management Center, Chicago, Illinois: "Trust and control seem to be two different ends of the spectrum. Boards desire to retain control; staff realizes that the more the board trusts the staff and task teams, the greater potential for release of control, resulting in the capacity to drive organizational performance. Bridging the gap between trust and control is a negotiated process. You must first establish your competence and reliability, then invest in the

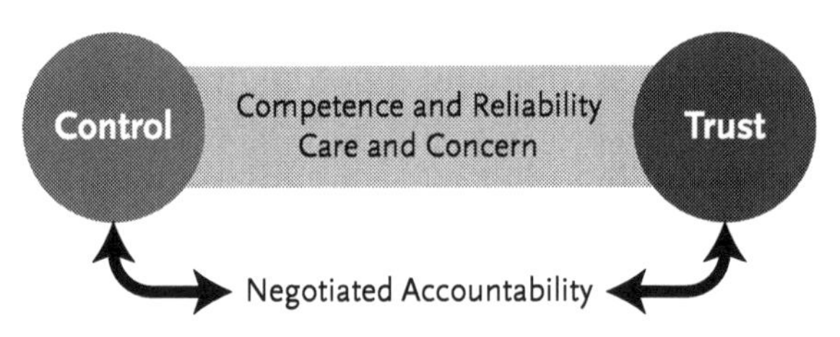

relationship element by showing authentic care and concern for individual leaders and the mission of the organization. Successfully bridging this gap is worth the journey."

Consider a Three-Lens Approach to Initiate and Guide Dialogues With Your Board

From Gary LaBranche, FASAE, CAE, president and CEO, Association for Corporate Growth, Chicago, Illinois: "Our success as CEOs is directly related to our ability to engage the imagination, support, and trust of board members. Creating a shared perspective is essential toward this end and requires an open mind and an open heart. To shape that understanding, I use a 'three-lens' approach to initiate and guide dialogue. The three lenses are:

- Stewardship (providing *oversight* to ensure the sustainable continuity of the association);
- Membership (providing *insight* to ensure the currency and relevancy of what the association does to meet and exceed member needs); and
- Leadership (providing *foresight* to ensure the future through new ideas, discovery, and innovation).

Only when we share a common framework for understanding do we have a chance at sharing a successful future together."

Keep the Dialogue Going

From Bob Stein, MBA, FASAE, CAE, president/CEO, American Society on Aging, San Francisco, California: "No board chair assumes his/her role with the intent to harm the organization. Keeping that in mind, listening and understanding, along with engaging in a continuous dialogue with the chair and the board is critical. Small problems can be averted this way. Big problems can be addressed in this way. I don't think there is a CEO who ever solved a problem with their board chair by retreating into silence when dissonance was present. A solid CEO and chair collaboration helps the organization ultimately achieve its mission with a business discipline rather than an emotional compass."

Lead, Communicate, and Shine

From Kerwin Brown, CAE, CEO/president, BEMA (Bakery Equipment Manufacturers and Allieds), Overland Park, Kansas: "When working with boards, I have kept in mind three simple words: lead, communicate, and shine.

Boards naturally are made up of leaders, but as CEOs, we need to do all we can to focus and direct those leaders to maximize their effectiveness. A push here, a suggestion there, and simple things like training on governance principles will help your board lead effectively.

Specific to communications, board members' memories are frequently short and not always accurate. Board meetings are typically months apart, participants can be distracted during meetings, and board members have real jobs they need to concentrate on. Board members often forget why strategic initiatives were passed or the exact numbers behind the justification of a new program or goal. Clear communication is often not simply one more email but hard and, most importantly, ongoing work. Lots of bad things can and will happen when board members collectively forget real facts and details. It's your job to remind them.

Finally, CEOs need to use their industry, media, and member connections to create shining moments for board members. Board self-assessment surveys frequently identify concerns about the lack of appreciation and recognition board members perceive they receive for the hundreds of hours they commit to their leadership roles. By helping them feel valued, you will motivate them to engage even more in their roles, to the benefit of the association."

Be the Historian Educator

From David Martin, CAE, CEO/executive vice president, Society of Critical Care Medicine, Mt. Prospect, Illinois: "It's key to remember that board members change regularly and you are a constant. This gives the CEO responsibility for providing an historical perspective during important board discussions, while reminding them you are not advocating for the past but simply explaining the history of the topic and former board decisions. In this same vein, the longtime CEO must constantly work to develop relationships and educate new board members. It's easy to think that the board knows certain things that happened several years ago, when in fact most of them may not because of regular board member turnover."

Educate to Accelerate

From Deborah J. Bowen, FACHE, FASAE, CAE, president and CEO, American College of Healthcare Executives, Chicago, Illinois: "Effective governance is critical to the success of any organization. Yet often we expect volunteers to understand how the board works without taking time to set the foundation. The most challenging part of any CEO's role is to ensure the collective talent and experience around the board table is used in the right way. For new board members that process begins well before the first board meeting with a good onboarding plan to set context and expectations. But it doesn't stop there. Change is the mantra of association work, so ongoing board education can help board members understand the effect of change on the industry, allowing time to look forward while honoring their oversight roles by monitoring results. Time is precious, and board members need to be armed with the right tools to ensure they can perform the work they came to do."

Communicate, Educate, and Relate

From Ed Salek, CAE, executive director, Society of Tribologists and Lubrication Engineers, Park Ridge, Illinois: "CEOs don't have much success if they think of their boards in the abstract—boxes on an organization chart or as anonymous faces that fill seats around a table. We are actually working with a group of individuals that comprise the governance body we call the board. Consequently, we have much more success when we do three things: communicate, educate, and relate. There is no such thing as too much board communication. Make sure board members feel that they are always being kept well-informed about the organization. Second, share your knowledge of how a successful association operates and be willing to speak up when your board might be off target. Finally, make a sincere effort to get to know individual board members and to understand their points of view. All three things are much easier said than done, especially if you are working with a large number of board members, but attention to them will pay dividends over time."

Demonstrate Level 5 Leadership

From Mark Golden, FASAE, CAE, executive director and corporate secretary, National Society of Professional Engineers, Alexandria, Virginia: "CEO effectiveness with volunteer leadership boards comes down to what Jim Collins called Level 5 leadership: 'the paradoxical blend of personal humility and [fierce] professional will.' You need to be able to take your own ego-gratification out of the equation when assessing the association's strategic needs but also refuse to make allowances for the board's limitations by compromising on the level of leadership their roles demand from them. You need to be authentic in giving the board credit for association success and in truly owning any board failure as your own. And never, never, never let a setback cause you to doubt yourself or become tentative and risk averse. Take the hit, learn what you can from it, turn the page and move on. In doing so, you not only become a safety net for the board, making it less risky for them to take bold action, but also model the behavior that will enable them to be effective in their own leadership roles."

Promoting Better Governance

Association CEOs have key roles to play to ensure the governance organizational structure and operations will best serve the association.

Lead in Building an Effective Governance Infrastructure

From Abe Eshkenazi, CSCP, CPA, FASAE, CAE, CEO, APICS, Chicago, Illinois: "Too often governance is viewed as an impediment to organizations and, specifically, the CEO's ability to achieve objectives. Boards generally reflect where the organization has been versus where it's going. The process used by many associations to select board officers and members reinforces this orientation—focusing on characteristics or criteria that are reflective of the past and the current board or 'people like us.' It's the CEO's responsibility to push for active management of governance, and it should be part of the annual evaluation process of goals and objectives. Boards are looking for leadership in governance and the association. CEOs are uniquely qualified to be a resource and provide leadership in this critical area."

Relentlessly Prowl for Future Leaders

From Stacy Brungardt, CAE, executive director, Society of Teachers of Family Medicine, Leawood, Kansas: "The CEO needs to ensure effective processes are in place to identify, select, and orient a diverse list of high quality leaders in key areas of their association's governance structure. You must relentlessly prowl for future leaders, track these stars, and move them into the board and committee structures when the opportunity arises. One concrete tactic is to maintain and regularly update a spreadsheet of potential future leaders with their key skills. This list can complement your open calls for committee, task force, and board openings and provide suggestions for quality leaders to fill these roles. The return on your attentiveness to this work will be invaluable."

Advocating for Members

Although board members are charged with representing an association's members, the CEO can play a key role in ensuring members' viewpoints are conveyed and considered.

Make Sure Your Board Knows What Members Need From the Association

From Thomas C. Dolan, PhD, FACHE, FASAE, CAE, executive coach/ consultant and president emeritus, American College of Healthcare Executives, Chicago, IL: "Board members often think they know what members need from the association based on what board members themselves need. But board members are typically more senior and successful than the average member. In addition, they are often influenced by a small number of vocal members. That is why it is important for you to ask a representative sample of members annually what they need from the association. It is especially powerful if you ask the association leaders the same questions and compare the responses."

Advocate for Grassroots Members

From Tom Marshall, executive director, American Association of Neurological Surgeons, Rolling Meadows, Illinois: "It is the CEO who can best speak for the collective membership in the boardroom. You and your staff collect and distill data identifying members' needs, understand the trends among the membership year in and year out, and keep your finger on the membership's pulse rate consistently, while board members turn over because of term limits.

I've always viewed the association CEO as the neck of a horizontal hourglass, with one end opening to the voices of the volunteer leadership and the other open to the voice of the grassroots member. In this way, the CEO can manage, assist, and facilitate the ebb and flow of needs, thoughts, and perceptions to ensure an effective choreography of goal, objective, process, and satisfaction—the lifeblood of effective associations."

Building Stronger Associations

Ultimately, CEOs need to team with their boards to lead associations into the future. Most associations simply cannot afford to remain stagnant.

Laser Focus on Your Mission

From Martin B. Tirado, CAE, CEO, Snow & Ice Management Association, Inc., Milwaukee, Wisconsin: "It's easy for association leaders and staff to take the mission of our association for granted. The mission, however, is a key differentiator in many ways. Use your mission to evaluate strategy decisions and become focused on what you do best. When hiring staff, remember people in the millennial generation want to make a difference in what they do in their careers. Make your mission a valued component to hiring and retaining this important sector of the workforce. Print your mission on board agendas and display it at your annual conference and in your office. These reminders will make you want to have a mission that is exciting and a central rallying point, as opposed to something buried in your board policies that rarely gets reviewed. In essence, by making your mission the focal point of everything you do, your association will become mission driven."

Challenge the Status Quo

From Robert Nelson, CAE, former president and CEO of the National Coffee Association and current CEO of Nelson Strategic Consulting, Washington, DC: "Great leaders are willing to challenge assumptions, both their own and, in a tactful manner, those of others and to dream about what's possible. One of your key roles as the CEO is to expand your learning and bring new ideas and concepts to the board. You must dare to do things differently, be willing to let go of long held beliefs and practices, and embrace calculated risk taking. You need to articulate a clear vision that stretches boundaries, while considering the board's latitude of acceptance. If you see yourself becoming too comfortable with what is, it's probably time to challenge the status quo and reach for what's possible."

Push Your Board

From Peter O'Neil, FASAE, CAE, former executive director of the American Industrial Hygiene Association, Falls Church, Virginia and current executive vice president and CEO of ASIS International, Alexandria, Virginia: "Boards are as good as their CEO helps them to be. At times CEOs do not do all they can to push their boards—perhaps because of poor working relationships, historical precedence, culture, or other factors. Boards assume the past dictates the future. But to quote Richard Bach, 'Argue for your limitations and sure enough they are yours.' If, for example, you fail to bring an innovative, potentially high ROI idea to the board because you perceive the board to be risk averse, you will have become the barrier or limitation to success. Challenge the past, challenge assumptions, and push your board to do what is right for the organization."

Be Prepared to Seize Opportunities

From Ronald S. Moen, MS, former CEO of four associations, most recently retired from the Society of Academic Emergency Medicine, Des Plaines, Illinois: "As the CEO of the association, you must be prepared to help the board and members seize opportunities when at first those opportunities may seem distant, difficult, or even impossible to achieve. Keeping in mind the strategic plan and the long-term vision of the association, don't become a slave to short-term objectives or existing programs, even if they seem to be fulfilling some of the members' needs. Numerous opportunities exist to create for-profit programs and companies that will support and foster the association and its members.

I know too many CEOs who are simply content to be followers and not visionaries for their associations. You are in the best position and are uniquely qualified to raise questions and to stimulate the board to think beyond what is current or available in the near term. The most successful associations are those whose leaders are constantly on the lookout to find new ways to meet member needs, to find profitable solutions to limited resources, and to be open to new and different ways to meet member needs. You should be able to finish your term, however short or long it may be, with confidence that the association is in a much better place than it was when you arrived."

Prioritize!

From Dr. Ron DeHaven, DVM, MBA, executive vice president/CEO, American Veterinary Medical Association, Schaumburg, Illinois: "Too many associations try to be all things to all members, often taking on pet projects or ideas coming from members without carefully evaluating how the membership will perceive, value, and use these products or services. Typically, new products and services are added but nothing is dropped. Peter Drucker said it well: 'It's easier for companies to come up with new ideas than to let go of the old ones.' The end result is a broad portfolio of 'good' products and services that have limited use, marginal value, and little awareness. You need to work with your board to ensure the association's products and services are limited to only those precious few that the membership says will be the most valuable to them, not what the board or you arbitrarily think will be the most valuable."

Remember the Three Ts in Deciding What to Do

From Mary Alexander, MA, RN, CRNI, FAAN, CAE, CEO, Infusion Nurses Society, Norwood, Massachusetts: "Boards want to make a difference for their organization. So they may want to initiate a project that, while potentially a worthy issue to address for the profession, may not be in alignment with the organization's mission or may conflict with the organization's current project completion dates. Since resources are limited, have the board consider the three Ts in deciding whether to go forward with a new initiative:

- *Time:* Will other projects be put on hold or abandoned to take on a new one? Is the timeline realistic for completion?
- *Talent:* Are there competent volunteers with knowledge and expertise who can complete this project on time? Is there adequate staff to support work of the volunteers?
- *Treasury:* What financial resources are needed to complete the work? Does the work fit in the budget?

Consideration of these key factors will help guide the board in making the decision that will be in the best interests of the association."

Final Thoughts for Association CEOs

Capping out this conglomeration of advice is input from two long-time friends of mine who are widely recognized in the association world. Each has more than 40 years of experience serving associations, including at least 30 years each as a CEO. Both are also fellows of ASAE.

Seven Keys to Success

From Dave Fellers, FASAE, CAE, former CEO of four associations and currently CEO of Dave Fellers Consulting, LLC, Prairie Village, Kansas: "In working with numerous association boards, I have found the most effective CEOs understand and have mastered the following areas:

1. Board development: This orientation should involve an annual refresher for both continuing and new board members about appropriate roles and how members should operate. Never assume board members know their roles versus your role and other staff.
2. Board self-assessment: Board assessment is as important as your own annual performance appraisal. Use one of many tools available in the market place, subsequently sharing your ideas about how to address areas of greatest concern during a board discussion.
3. Next generation member awareness: Make sure board members understand the interests and needs of younger members and prospects. All too often, associations will conduct great member needs surveys, but they don't adequately discuss the results and what the surveys tell them, especially related to younger members' needs.
4. Governance structure: Periodically facilitate board discussions about the governance structure (e.g., board size, committee structure, roles and responsibilities). What's right now may not be right a few years down the road in meeting the association's needs.
5. Board succession plan: Make sure the board realizes its role in identifying, recruiting, and developing future leaders, and do your part in grooming future leaders.
6. Staff succession plan: Develop and periodically refresh your own succession plan as well as plans for other key staff, for the board's future reference. The board needs to be ready to act in the event you leave the association and to have confidence that you're ready to act if one of your key staff leaves.

7. Board ambassador coaching: Use board members as effective liaisons and ambassadors for the association, providing guidance about how to 'wave the flag' and their roles and obligations to increase the awareness and brand of the organization.

Although there are certainly other key CEO roles, I have found a CEO's mastery of these seven frequently distinguish the best from the mediocre."

Tough Love: 10 Lessons From the Trenches

From Chris Mahaffey, MS, FASAE, CAE, executive director, American College of Foot and Ankle Surgeons, Chicago, Illinois: "Although there are many attributes that correspond with success as an association CEO, following are 10 that stand out to me:

- Being a good CEO is more of an 'art' in human relations than it is a 'science' in management.
- Stick to your mission. Do a few things well, not a lot half-baked.
- Practice what you preach and be consistent. The precedents you set are critical.
- Boards are not motivated by what motivates you. Boards are motivated by altruism and esteem. You are motivated by safety and physiological needs. (See Maslow's *Hierarchy of Needs.*) Be attuned to the differences at all times.
- Differentiate your organization from the competition, even if that means fewer dollars or members.
- Don't let the 'tail wag the dog.' Example: Focus on your primary members. Without the primary members, the secondary members won't join anyway.
- Pick your battles carefully. But if there's one thing to battle, its member conflicts of interests. They harm decision making and your organization's reputation.
- Get an 'evergreen' employment agreement. You're either hired or fired. 'Terms' are an anachronism from the profession's early days. Expiration dates just invite problems.
- Trust the advice of people who've walked in your shoes. We are awash in 'experts' who have little if any experience being on the firing line.
- And most importantly, if you have grown because of someone, help someone grow because of you."

And the Buck Stops With...

Board members, the board chair, and the CEO have plenty of practical advice to chew on in this chapter from more than 30 experienced association leaders who contributed to it.

As association leaders, you can't incorporate every piece of this advice in your leadership role. Choose no more than five items to focus on that match best with the specific challenges you are facing and the operating environment you work in.

Tying It Back to the Members

Throughout this book, my focus has been on doing what is best for an association's members. Board directors, other member leaders, and staff are stewards of their association, ensuring its mission and vision are attained and that the most possible value is delivered to members by a staff and infrastructure that is strong and vibrant. Every action taken and every decision made should have this stewardship in mind.

SECTION 4

Moving Forward

CHAPTER 12

Take Comfort That Change Is Possible: Leadership Success Stories to Guide You

I HAVE COVERED A LOT OF ground identifying opportunities to improve association leadership: The need to better prepare, continually educate, and manage performance of association member leaders. The need to appropriately assign roles and responsibilities to all the various governance entities and the staff. The value of good relationships with an association's key stakeholders. The crucial role of strategic planning and how member and staff leaders should interact to develop, implement, monitor, and continually fine-tune plans to maximize their ROIs. The frequently ignored fiduciary responsibility boards have to monitor and manage organizational risk. Perhaps most critical, the importance of strong working relationships between the CEO and the board and its officers.

Giving attention to these and other critical ingredients of organizational success can pay significant dividends. Even though the process of transforming association leadership practices and mindsets may seem daunting, it is entirely possible. This book concludes with a few real case studies that collectively illustrate successful, multiyear journeys to excellence, told by individuals who have experienced the journey first-hand. I hope they will serve as role models for you.

Case Study 1—Healthcare Information and Management Systems Society (HIMSS), Chicago, Illinois

From Steve Lieber, CAE, President and CEO

Going into the search process in 1999 for a new staff leader, HIMSS was financially strong, had a stable base of members, and had achieved a measure of success with its primary educational event. In short, significant change was not required; in fact, the easy path was for the organization to keep doing what it had been doing. Yet, the governance-management relationship was not ideal, with the board straying too much into addressing operational issues. That status quo included a governance-management relationship that included such things as the following:

- The board made numerous business decisions, including site locations for events and pricing decisions for products and services provided by the society.
- Each year the incoming president, a member-elected volunteer, would announce his or her "agenda."
- The executive director was charged with performing administrative tasks and ensuring operational logistics were implemented.
- There were minimal expectations of staff having in-depth knowledge of subjects pertaining to society management; that was the purview of the volunteer members.
- In summary, true governance at the board level was largely unknown and true business acumen at the management level was limited by board policies of approval and executive limitations.

These points are not always indicative of an association in danger. But they are characteristics that can stymie and limit the future of an organization.

Several directors of the HIMSS board in 1999 believed that the structure and roles currently played by the board and staff needed to change if the organization was to realize its true potential. They recognized that the board should stop being a board of managers and be what their title was, a true board of directors. They also recognized that they needed a president and CEO—not an executive director. To them, these were not simply word changes but fundamental shifts in the roles of people and changes in the influence of the board and the management executive.

In early 2000, I was hired as president and CEO. The board chair (That title had been changed from president several years earlier.) explicitly told me why they had renamed the management executive title: "We believe this title (president and CEO) means something." The message was, "We expect you to lead." The chair and his colleagues were also clear that they wanted to become a board of directors, not managers, and wanted the president and CEO to help them get there.

Over the course of my first year, not in major actions but through evolutionary steps, the board and I began to find our places. In most cases, the board made statements like, "You are management, we're not; your decision," and would call out any board member who "started to get into the weeds." In other cases, I simply acted on the authority that I believed they had given me—an "act now, ask forgiveness later" approach. While I never asked for forgiveness, there were a few bumps along the way. In my second year, the chair (a new one every year) and I came to verbal blows over my independence. However, he picked the wrong area to come after me—management authority and independence. The rest of the board came down on this issue without wavering from their original intent: a president and CEO must have management authority and independence. Their position was that management is held to measurable metrics and then given the discretion about how to get there.

That led to a guiding principle we still use today; the board says "why" and the CEO says "how." I have maintained a clear understanding that I do not set the society's positions; that is a board of directors' function. I do not shy away from making management decisions, but I think remembering the difference between position decisions and management decisions is a career-lengthening distinction to retain.

While the role of management began to change to one of greater business autonomy and authority, the role of the board also changed. It was my job to not allow operational topics on the board's agenda and to make sure that the board continually engaged in strategic and big picture discussions at every board meeting, not just every three years.

Governance oversight was defined through a comprehensive metrics set, measured, and reviewed regularly, which replaced board management of projects and tactics. Committee reports also disappeared from the board agendas, given they were too tactical and operational; staff reports of outcomes replaced them. The board came to recognize, and does still today, that their value is their knowledge and expertise resulting from their current engagement in the field. But they also are cognizant of their limitations. They are not the ones with the full-time HIMSS jobs—staff has those.

This evolved view of staff roles represents one of the most significant changes I have experienced during my tenure. First, there is now an unlimited endorsement of headquarters staff expertise and competency; the board knows that the people who are on the job every day need to know the business. My role as president and CEO, along with the roles of other staff, came to be more than business managers; we are seen as major partners in strategic management.

Several years into my tenure, a vice chair said to me, "Steve, never come into the board room with a blank sheet of paper." I believe this statement is in full support of the one made to me when hired to "lead." So while the board and I fully embrace the governance principle that the board sets strategic direction, they do it in partnership with management. Again, because we work every day on HIMSS business, staff is attuned to both the current and future worlds facing the society. Therefore, the staff is where the strategic ideation and initial analysis usually begin, followed by board discussion and guidance, further analysis and adapting by staff, and final shaping and decision making by the board.

So what have been the results?

- FY00 total revenues were $10M; FY14 total revenues were $84M.
- FY00 membership stood at 12,000; FY14 membership was 57,000 members.
- In FY00, 74 percent of HIMMS revenue came from the annual meeting, 12 percent from membership, 8 percent from publications and other education, and 6 percent from investment income. By FY14, revenue streams were much more diversified, with 47 percent coming from the annual meeting, 11 percent from membership, 15 percent from data services, 14 percent from media services, 10 percent from non-U.S. operations, and 3 percent from investment income. This diversification helps protect the society from unpredictable and uncontrollable swings in profitability associated with the annual meeting.
- There were 32 staff in 2000, compared to just under 400 in 2014.
- In 2000, there was one office in Chicago; now there are five offices in the United States, two in Germany, one in England, and one in Singapore.
- The association went from one governing body in 2000 to a multiboard governance model in 2014, with separate governing bodies for North America, Europe, and Asia. The media and data analytics business unit also has a separate governance board.

Is there cause and effect here? Certainly not entirely. We cannot completely attribute these positive outcomes to the change in governance/management philosophy. HIMSS has benefited from a drastically changed external environment that has provided us with business opportunities that did not exist in 2000, which would have much to do with the above successes. But I do believe the organizational philosophy of management leadership, innovation, risk taking, and authority under a constructive governance oversight of objective metrics, strategic engagement, partnership, and delegation is what made the magnitude of the successes possible.

Case Study 2—American Industrial Hygiene Association (AIHA), Falls Church, Virginia

From Peter O'Neil, FASAE, CAE, former AIHA Executive Director and current Executive Vice President and CEO of ASIS International, Alexandria, Virginia

By any measure available, AIHA is an outstanding organization. This is true today, and it was true over a decade ago when I was hired for the first of what would be three different positions in the organization.

As I began my career as AHIA's group leader, marketing and membership, I quickly realized that the relationships among volunteers, board and staff were not strong. In fact, they bordered on toxic! I recall thinking at the time that if a member of the senior staff, including the executive director, were to have told the board or another volunteer leader the sky was blue that day, the party on the receiving end of that data point would likely have walked to the nearest window to look.

Nearly 13 years later, after a lot of effort, soul searching, professional development for staff and volunteers, and a major organizational culture change—all planned, coordinated, and implemented in a deliberate, purposed, and well-crafted fashion—AIHA thrives.

How did this transformation occur, and how have we sustained it over time? In our case, the case for change came early in the new millennium with the retirement of our tenured CEO. In thinking about the association's future needs, several influential board members concluded it was not "fun" to serve on the board and took way too much of their time. These feelings began to spread among the board. AIHA's new executive director, who had been the deputy executive director, and I, the newly promoted deputy, decided it was time to act.

We sat down with key members of the board, some tenured and others in their first year, and laid out for them what AIHA could be and could do with a major overhaul of culture, governance, and, candidly, staff who were then viewed as obstacles rather than contributors to the organization's success. After several discussions, we began our journey.

The journey was long and was not always easy. For example, purposely and deliberately we identified employees who simply would not or could not fit into the new culture and organization we intended to build. So we actively "coached out" these employees by helping them see the "fit" was no longer there. This process involved some tough, honest conversations, but even the most tenured who needed to leave ultimately did with little or no difficulty. We had our fair share of challenges around this staff reorganization, but I am proud to say we did not lose a single employee that we intended to keep during this time, and our capacity as a staff grew exponentially every time we brought in a new person—and a corresponding new perspective.

AIHA has accomplished a lot over the past 13 years. Chief among these accomplishments are:

- Creation and maintenance of a climate of trust among and between volunteers, board, and staff, including implementation of a board and staff "speak with one voice" policy. Such a climate was in part achieved by the changes we were willing to make with our staff and the changes the AIHA board was willing to make. The board's "speak with one voice" policy basically states that once all parties are included in a deliberation and a decision is made, the board will publicly support the vote. This "policy" holds to this day and the culture of the board actively works to ensure it survives.
- Reorganized governance of AIHA. We created three limited liability companies to strengthen and distinguish businesses we operate from the core 501(c)(6) organization. This move streamlined operations, made decision making in the three new entities more nimble, and ultimately contributed to significant growth. It also freed the AHIA board to concentrate more attention on its core mission of advocating and providing educational opportunities for members.
- Decreased the size of our board from 16 to 13, while giving members more opportunities to participate in our technical committee structure.
- Implementation of a volunteer leadership development program in which volunteers, especially board members, are educated about their roles and responsibilities. We actively use ASAE's CEO Symposium and Exceptional Boards programs to train our board members. These two programs have proven enormously useful in helping me help our leadership understand who "steers" and who "rows" the association ship. Further, we have a very good, two-and-a-half-day annual board orientation program, and we pair new board members with tenured board members in every board meeting.

- An ongoing commitment to actively manage our human talent and to actively coach staff. This includes coaching them out when necessary. I see this as one of my primary responsibilities, and I am fortunate to have an incredible chief human resource officer with whom I partner. I make it a point to have a relationship with every staff person and to ensure they do not misunderstand that relationship. I also make it a point to ensure our end-implementers, not just senior staff, are in key meetings. Including a broader array of staff in such meetings has proven invaluable to me.
- A completely redesigned product service delivery model and, as a result, our business model (in process). AIHA has moved over the past several years from a technical committee-driven culture to an organization-driven content strategy culture, including formal and informal research as well as more input from a broader spectrum of stakeholder groups than ever before. This cultural change has been a challenge, but I have helped our board realize that it is the key to AIHA's next 75 years of success.

Our work is not done. We strive every day to protect what we have built and to bring countless others along with us. We stumble and sometimes we fail, but we have a culture that understands what's important and what's not. And that counts for a lot.

Case Study 3—Michigan Society of Association Executives (MSAE), East Lansing, Michigan

From Cheryl Ronk, FASAE, CAE, Executive Director

A major shift occurred within MSAE approximately 20 years ago. Before then, the organization was fairly traditional, with a portfolio of products, programs, and services that mirrored those of similar societies in other states. The board generally embraced the status quo—tinkering here and there but not thinking and acting strategically or embracing creativity in serving the organization and its members.

With a change in board leadership, and with my prompting, the board decided to move in a new direction. This included embracing a knowledge-based governance model—a core of governance training within the CAE program. There was a mindset of collecting and sharing knowledge to determine MSAE's goals and objectives. A priority was placed on listening to members and monitoring trends. All board members were trained about this model and have been retrained as needed.

The new direction also included driving a culture of implementing best practices internally and identifying new out-of-the-box programs to grow and strengthen MSAE. This was a huge obligation for the organization, but one that was embraced by all.

Following are some specific things we did and continue to do to strengthen the board/staff partnership and drive organizational success:

1. We work hard to identify and recruit thought leaders to fill board seats. We want directors who embrace questioning, investigating, setting goals and objectives, and taking calculated risks. We seek out individuals who don't shy away from doing work and being inclusive.
2. Staff members make concerted efforts to support a strategically focused board. We continually do everything possible to ensure board members are educated and prepared to act strategically during and between board meetings.
3. The board has embraced a culture of owning its work. For example, when considering a new program or direction, board members typically engage in hearty discussions on their risk tolerance. They treat MSAE's assets as they would their own. Not everything we have done has been fruitful, but we have learned from every experience.
4. After the board sets goals and objectives, it allows the staff and committees to be entrepreneurial in identifying and implementing strategies and tactics. Specific to committees, we take care to recruit members with the right expertise who will provide the greatest benefit for their efforts. We do not wait for a member to volunteer. In fact, we often add experts in the field to committees even if they are not members. Staff and members discuss who would be best for specific initiatives and we invite them to participate. Using the best to guide the best has led to our innovative and creative culture.
5. We keep the mission current and let it drive the decision-making process. The mission leads to a preferred future and a current strategic plan that drives our annual scope of work through the budget process and committee structure with specific outcome statements. We are now expanding this focus on mission to set our annual organizational and personal goals as well.

The board/staff partnership has led to considerable success for MSAE in implementing a number of unique programs.

For example, we embraced adult learning and a professional development model. We used to have monthly meeting groups featuring a "sage on the stage" with lunch. Considering participant feedback, we shifted to education that was learner centric and based on what our members needed at various levels of their careers. Programs were specifically designed for those entering the field, those emerging, for dynamic leaders, and those leaving a legacy.

After the professional development model was successfully implemented, MSAE started taking additional risks. We put our CAE preparation program online and used best practices for virtual learning. Over time, we have grown this program to include more than 110 participants annually from virtually every state, with one of the highest CAE exam pass rates of any preparation program.

We instigated an executive search service, which is fairly unique for our type of association. It benefits not only our own members but other associations and job candidates from around the country. We use selection criteria gleaned from the top 100 elements of success needed to be successful in the sector.

Additional innovations driven by our strategically focused board and staff include a resource library, a lobbying and political action compliance program, an organizational membership category, and a "party with a purpose" that replaced the trade show while keeping buyers informed about new developments with suppliers. MSAE always has three to five initiatives or priorities for the year—not too many, but enough to keep us fresh.

MSAE certainly has had its share of strife, conflicts, and challenges over time. We had a major shift when staff was first hired and responsibilities had to be sorted out between the board and staff. There was a time when the board was doing or redoing committee work, and we had to identify and rectify the situation. We have had major, spirited discussions on the level of risk and investment MSAE would take on new initiatives. We have discussed what strategic discussion is as well as our work and how it affects our brand.

However, one of the major assets of MSAE is that the board manages itself. The board members discuss their culture and they hold each other accountable. As association executives themselves, they are accustomed to sitting in my chair, as the chief staff executive. They remind each other that they are board members and have a different role.

Bottom line, how you think is how you lead, so get great thinkers in leadership roles. Respect their ideas and allow them to lead together. Facilitate future environmental scanning and share findings. Foster the respect within the staff for listening to others and not discounting something that may be uncomfortable or foreign to you. Create common desired outcomes (ends statements), clarify values, and investigate. Look for diversity of thought and agree on key success measures. Study and make the organization a learning organization where there are established rules of engagement, a high performing board, and a staff that supports a strategic board.

CHAPTER 13

How Do You Stack Up?

THE INTRODUCTION TO THIS BOOK advised association leaders to prioritize among all recommendations ones that offer the best return on whatever time and other resources are available. This advice is reinforced now at the end. You simply cannot do everything at once.

Following is a tool you may want to consider in starting the prioritization process. It includes a listing of key recommendations from each chapter, with an opportunity for you to assess how you stack up relative to each one. Once your assessment is completed, your board and the CEO should collaborate to identify which items will be initially prioritized for action. Then go to it—for the good of the members!

Chapter 1: Maximize Member Leader Competency

Recommendations	Not Yet Addressed	Improve	We're Role Models
Ensure candidates for board and other leadership positions demonstrate at least a minimum understanding of the organization and the related fiduciary responsibilities associated with their roles before being placed on the ballot or notified of their appointment.			
Provide newly elected and appointed leaders access to orientation documents before the start of their service and require attestation of their being read.			

Recommendations	Not Yet Addressed	Improve	We're Role Models
Give newly elected and appointed leaders an opportunity to attend one or more meetings of their assigned entity before the start of their service.			
Facilitate an in-person board orientation before the start of the new leaders' terms of office.			
Administer customized orientations for new officers.			
Ensure the incoming board chair attends an external orientation program with the CEO (e.g., one of the ASAE programs).			
Institute a mentorship program to supplement the formal orientation program during the first year of service on a governance entity.			
Undertake periodic needs assessments to identify priorities for board member continuing education.			
Allocate time on all or selected board meeting agendas for continuing education, based on assessed needs.			
Complete assessments at the end of each board meeting to elicit perceptions of the meeting and participants.			
Undertake year-end assessments of the board and committees as entities.			
Assign the role of governance coach to the immediate past president or another respected member leader.			

Chapter 2: Assign Roles to Those Best Suited

Recommendations	Not Yet Addressed	Improve	We're Role Models
Identify and inventory typical roles and decisions that require input or involvement from multiple governance entities, specific officer positions, and staff.			

Recommendations	Not Yet Addressed	Improve	We're Role Models
Assign and document roles and decision-making authority to the right entities and positions. It's clear who has ultimate accountability for making decisions, who needs to be involved, and who needs to be notified.			
Include role and decision-making matrices as a core component of new board member orientation as well as continuing education.			
Ensure role and decision-making accountabilities are appropriately addressed in the following areas, which are frequently subject to excessive involvement by volunteer leaders: • Human resource management; • Meeting management; • Marketing management; and • Public and media relations management.			

Chapter 3: Understand Your Basic Fiduciary Duties

Recommendations	Not Yet Addressed	Improve	We're Role Models
Understand what the duty of care means.			
Understand what the duty of loyalty means.			
Understand what the duty of obedience means.			

Chapter 4: Select and Onboard Your CEO the Right Way

Recommendations	Not Yet Addressed	Improve	We're Role Models
Make the right staff leadership decision during the transition period.			
Have defined criteria for selecting search committee members.			
Use a professional search firm to hire your next CEO, unless there is a clear heir-apparent within the association.			
Hire the best search firm to meet your needs.			

Recommendations	Not Yet Addressed	Improve	We're Role Models
Devote sufficient time to the CEO recruitment process.			
Achieve true consensus (not just lip service) about the desired CEO profile before launching a search for candidates.			
Avoid limiting the CEO candidate pool, including a requirement that the CEO be from the profession or trade.			
Strategize CEO compensation to attract the best candidates: • Define the appropriate competitive market. • Target overall compensation, along with specific compensation components, in line with the market.			
Ask the right questions when interviewing CEO candidates.			
Be transparent with information to CEO candidates.			
Maintain confidentiality with regard to search committee deliberations.			
Commit to comprehensive CEO onboarding that includes: • Completion of pre-hire key stakeholder assessments; • Implementation of a good communication plan; • Establishment of a transition team; • Clarification of board/CEO roles and communication protocols; • Jump starting the chair/CEO working relationship; • Clarification of board/staff relationship protocols; and • Establishment of initial performance expectations.			

Chapter 5: Nurture the CEO/Board Working Relationship

Recommendations	Not Yet Addressed	Improve	We're Role Models
Adhere to a comprehensive CEO performance management process that includes: • Performance planning; • Mid-year assessment; • Year-end assessment; and • Ties to compensation decisions.			
Stick to agreed-upon roles for officers, governance entities, and staff.			
Foster transparent communication built on a foundation of trust and mutual respect (i.e., the Golden Rule) between the board and CEO.			
Ensure that the topic of board/CEO communication is periodically included as a board meeting agenda item.			
CEO communicates effectively with the board and its officers. (Consider tips offered in this book by your colleagues.)			
CEO nurtures individual relationships with • High potential leaders before their serving on the board; • Board members; • Officers not in the chair progression; • Chair-elect; and • Chair.			

Chapter 6: Strive for Win/Win Stakeholder Relationships

Recommendations	Not Yet Addressed	Improve	We're Role Models
Encourage and support a continuous program of member research to understand the needs and desires of members.			
Provide opportunities for members to engage with your association to the extent they have interest in doing so.			
Ensure the committee/work team selection process is as fair, open, and inclusive as possible.			

Recommendations	Not Yet Addressed	Improve	We're Role Models
Establish and periodically review a corporate relations strategy.			
Board members make staff aware of relationships they have with current and potential corporate partners.			
Board members team as requested by staff to build and nurture relationships with current and potential corporate partners.			
Monitor corporate partner satisfaction levels.			
Inventory and prioritize the best organizational partnerships to add member value.			
Craft and implement strategies to nurture relationships with top priority organizations.			
Value and build a board/staff partnership in serving the association and its members.			
Ensure a human resources audit is undertaken periodically by the association's attorney or a reputable consulting firm.			
Support employee training and development, professional certification, and participation by staff in professional associations.			
Monitor staff turnover levels and reasons for turnover.			
Encourage the association's pursuit of recognition as an employer of choice.			
Avoid excessive reliance on individual staff in forming impressions of staff engagement and morale.			

Chapter 7: Plan for Future Success

Recommendations	Not Yet Addressed	Improve	We're Role Models
Ensure a strong board/staff partnership in crafting your strategic plan.			

Recommendations	Not Yet Addressed	Improve	We're Role Models
Undertake environmental scanning prior to strategic plan development.			
Create white space for new initiatives by critically reviewing and paring down current products, programs, and services.			
Focus on a few key strategic priorities, as opposed to a laundry list of initiatives.			
Avoid a flavor-of-the-year mentality.			
Link strategic with operational planning.			
Assign accountability for plan attainment.			
Continually monitor and report progress on plan milestones.			
Include all staff in incentive plans that reward attainment of plan goals and milestones.			
Be willing to add, delete, and modify plan goals and initiatives if the operating environment changes.			

Chapter 8: Identify and Manage Risks

Recommendations	Not Yet Addressed	Improve	We're Role Models
Inventory organizational risks.			
Categorize and prioritize risks using a balanced scorecard approach.			
Develop abatement strategies for high priority risks.			
Document and periodically update a risk management matrix.			
Make risk management a recurring board meeting agenda item.			
Ensure your association maintains and periodically tests a business continuity plan.			
Ensure your association maintains and periodically reviews a key event cancellation plan			

Recommendations	Not Yet Addressed	Improve	We're Role Models
Ensure your association maintains and periodically updates a staff leadership succession plan.			
Ensure your association maintains and periodically updates a crisis communication plan.			

Chapter 9: Share With and Learn From Your Colleagues

Recommendations	Not Yet Addressed	Improve	We're Role Models
Support and prioritize involvement by the CEO and other staff in their professional societies.			
Attend ASAE and related society educational and networking events.			
Identify and cultivate peer groups in the association community for benchmarking purposes.			
Be willing to share information as well as ask for help.			
Follow the benchmarking code of conduct.			

Chapter 10: Heed Advice From Your Attorney

Recommendations	Not Yet Addressed	Improve	We're Role Models
Board Members			
Represent the organization as a whole, not specific constituencies.			
Rein in Napoleonic chairs.			
Avoid lazy board syndrome by ensuring all board members are attuned to their fiduciary responsibilities.			
Build trust with members by maintaining open lines of communication.			
Divulge and truly manage conflicts of interest.			

Recommendations	Not Yet Addressed	Improve	We're Role Models
Protect the organization's financial assets, with board members holding themselves to the "prudent person" standard.			
Do not get too personal with staff.			
Know who can speak for the board.			
Refrain from micromanaging committees.			
Do not misuse your organizational title.			
Know and appreciate for whom your attorney works.			
Don't let your attorney overstep her/his role.			
CEOs			
Lead your board from behind.			
Don't shortchange getting legal opinions to save a few dollars.			
Strategically time requests for your personal benefit.			

Chapter 11: Consider Food for Thought From Experienced CEOs

Recommendations	Not Yet Addressed	Improve	We're Role Models
Board Members			
Be your association's evangelists.			
Focus on the strategic plan.			
Combat the "are we a member-driven or staff-driven association" argument.			
Engage all board members in discussions.			
Challenge erroneous statements made by board colleagues.			
Lead your colleagues toward a generative mindset.			
CEOs			
Really get to know your board members.			
Engage with each individual board member.			

Recommendations	Not Yet Addressed	Improve	We're Role Models
Focus on building trust with board members.			
Bridge the gap between trust and control with your board.			
Consider a three-lens approach of providing oversight, insight, and foresight to initiate and guide dialogues with your board.			
Keep the dialogue going with board members rather than backing off when dissonance is present.			
Be an historian educator.			
Educate board members at all stages of their involvement.			
Demonstrate a blend of personal humility and fierce professional will (level 5 leadership).			
Lead in building an effective governance infrastructure.			
Relentlessly prowl for future leaders.			
Make sure your board knows what members need from the association.			
Advocate for the grassroots members.			
Laser focus on your mission.			
Challenge the status quo.			
Push your board.			
Be prepared to seize opportunities.			
Prioritize what you do; avoid trying to do everything for everyone.			
Consider the availability of time, talent, and treasury (the 3 T's) in making decisions for undertaking new initiatives.			

Appendices

APPENDIX 1.1

Sample Board Orientation Manual Categories and Topics

Following is a sample manual taxonomy. It is comprehensive, and it advisable to highlight a subset of documents for special attention. Incoming board members should formally attest that they have read and understand the contents of these documents. Accountability for updating each manual document should be assigned to a specific individual, in some cases a board member and in other cases a staff person. There should also be a defined frequency for reviewing and updating documents, which could vary from semiannually to triannually depending on the extent of anticipated changes over time.

Section 1: Setting the Context

Agenda Item	Update Accountability	Update Frequency
Historical Overview of the Association		
Key Milestones		
Past Chairs		
Code of Ethics		

Section 2: Governance Organization, Roles, and Rosters

Agenda Item	Update Accountability	Update Frequency
Governance Structure/Flowchart Diagram		
Governance Matrix		
Bylaws		
Officer Roles, Responsibilities, and Calendars		
Board Member Roles, Responsibilities, and Roster		
Committee Charters, Current Charges, and Rosters		
Committee Roles: Chair, Member, and Staff Liaison		
Representatives to Other Organizations—Roles, Charges, and Rosters		

Section 3: Staff Organization and Roles

Agenda Item	Update Accountability	Update Frequency
Staff Organization Chart		
Staff Telephone Directory		
Who to Contact for What		
Department Overviews: Roles and Key Outputs for Each Department		

Section 4: Board Meeting Management

Agenda Item	Update Accountability	Update Frequency
Historical Overview		
Board Meeting Schedule		
Board Agenda/Materials: • Recurring Meeting Agenda Items • Dates and Deadlines for Agenda Material Submission • Agenda Structure and Sample • How to Submit an Agenda Item		
Parliamentary Procedures		

Agenda Item	Update Accountability	Update Frequency
Board Minutes: • Format • Prior Year Meeting Minutes		
Board Travel: • Booking Arrangements • Expense Reimbursement Policy • Expense Reimbursement Form • International Travel Policy		

Section 5: Board Productivity and Effectiveness

Agenda Item	Update Accountability	Update Frequency
Duties and Responsibilities of Not-for-Profit Directors		
Principles of Good Governance and Ethical Practice		
Board Buddy Role and Expectations		
Being an Effective Board Member		
Board Member Obligations: • Code of Conduct • Conflicts of Interest • Confidentiality • Board Ethics • Communication Agreements		
Email Protocols		
Conference Call Etiquette		
Interacting Appropriately with the Media		
Distinguishing Governance Versus Operations—Case Studies		
Ground Rules for Board/Staff Interactions		
Ground Rules for Board/Journal Interactions		

Section 6: Strategy and Policy Role

Agenda Item	Update Accountability	Update Frequency
Strategic Planning Committee: Roles and Responsibilities		
Strategic Plan Development Calendar		
Current Strategic Plan		
Milestones Reporting Format		
Governance Policies: Complete Set		

Section 7: Accountability Role

Agenda Item	Update Accountability	Update Frequency
Financial Management: • Fiscal Year • Budget Development Cycle • Current Year Budget • Year-to-Date Financial Results • Interpreting the Balance Sheet and Income Statement • Accounting Procedures • Investment Policy		
CEO Performance Management: • Process Description • Current Year Performance Metrics • Assessment Form		

Section 8: Positioning and Alignment Role

Agenda Item	Update Accountability	Update Frequency
Government Affairs Committee: Role and Responsibilities		
Public Policy Agenda		
Current Position Statements		
Current Coalition Partners		
Government Relations Resources		

Section 9: Risk Management and Legal Compliance Role

Agenda Item	Update Accountability	Update Frequency
Risk Management Matrix		
Previous Year Audit Report and Management Letter		
Insurance Policies: • Business and Property Insurance • Directors and Officers Liability Insurance • Business Travel Accident Insurance • Meeting Cancelation Insurance • Medical Benefits Abroad Insurance		
Whistleblower Policy		
Intermediate Sanctions Compliance: • Compensation Strategy • Previous Year Demonstrated Strategy Compliance		

Section 10: Key Information

Agenda Item	Update Accountability	Update Frequency
Organization's Metrics Performance		
Current Year Member Survey		
Knowledge Warehouse		

APPENDIX 1.2

Sample Board Orientation Meeting Agenda Template

Following is a sample agenda template that assumes an initial time block geared exclusively to new members and a second time block that includes all board members.

New Board Members Only Session

Time	Agenda Items	Facilitator
	Call to Order and Review of Meeting Agenda	Incoming Chair
	Historical Perspective of the Organization: • What you need to know • Key historical milestones that still affect board operations and dynamics	Governance Coach
	Hopes and Expectations for You as a Board Member	Incoming Chair and CEO
	Governance Structure: • Officer roles • Board member roles • Committee structure and roles • Affiliated organization (e.g., Foundation) interactions	CEO
	Distinguishing Governance From Operations—One or Two Case Studies	Governance Coach
	Fiduciary and Ethical Responsibilities	Attorney
	Financial Oversight Deep Dive: • External perspective • Internal perspective • How to review and interpret the organization's financial statements	 Audit Firm Leader Treasurer CFO

Time	Agenda Items	Facilitator
	Staff Relations: • Overviews of each department • Ground rules of board/staff interactions	CEO
	Board Customs and Expectations—Dos and Don'ts Beyond the Orientation Manual	Governance Coach
	Setting the Stage for Your Success: • Leveraging your mentor relationship • How to be viewed as an effective contributor	Governance Coach
	General Q&A and Wrap-Up	CEO

Lunch with Entire Board and Staff Executives

All Board Members Session

Time	Agenda Items	Facilitator
	Call to Order and Review of Meeting Agenda	Incoming Chair
	Board Team-Building Exercise	Governance Coach
	Board Vision for Upcoming Year	Incoming Chair
	Review and Discuss Previous Year Board Self-Evaluation and Future Implications	Governance Coach
	Review and Discuss Upcoming Year Board Education Agenda	CEO
	Review and Discuss the Organization's Most Recent Business Risk Assessment	CEO
	General Q&A and Wrap-Up	Incoming Chair

APPENDIX 1.3

Sample Board Development Needs Survey

Following are categorized lists of competencies and skills which, in most associations, would be helpful for board members to have in fulfilling their roles. At least annually, board members should be asked to assess their knowledge level for each of these via a survey instrument. The results should influence completion of an annual calendar of board education.

Consider using the following five-point scale in assessing competency and skill attainment:

5 = Expert, could help others
4 = Good knowledge and understanding of the content
3 = Neutral, have average knowledge of the topic
2 = Know basics, need more information for better understanding
1 = Limited experience or knowledge in this area

Governance and Operations Topics

1. Process for board and staff decision making;
2. Board member legal obligations and responsibilities;
3. Board member fiduciary responsibilities;
4. The organization's bylaws and policies;
5. Board's role in the performance evaluation of the CEO;
6. Roles and responsibilities of board committees (Governance, Finance, etc.);
7. Role and rules for executive sessions of the board.

Finance

1. Financial reports presented by the treasurer and finance department, including balance statements, income and expenses, and other periodic reports;
2. The organization's investment policies and related decision making.

Effective Use of Technology

1. How to access and effectively navigate the members-only and board-only sections of the website;
2. Handling and organizing large volumes of email.

Accountability

1. Familiarity with the organization's conflict of interest policy;
2. Confidentiality issues regarding board discussions and executive sessions.

Parliamentary Procedure

1. Basics of parliamentary procedure;
2. Parliamentary procedure during board meetings;
3. Procedure to be followed in the recording and approval of minutes.

Strategic Direction

1. The role of the board in the strategic planning process;
2. The process for the organization's strategic and operating plans to guide resource allocation;
3. The process for how strategic and operating milestones are tracked and reported.

Mapping the Future

Use the following five-point scale in identifying importance of the following topics in board education and development:

5 = Very high priority
4 = High priority
3 = Neutral
2 = Low priority
1 = Very low priority

Potential board education and development topics:

1. Trends in association management;
2. Leadership development before members reach leadership positions;

3. Training in global thinking;
4. Training on interacting with the media;
5. Clarification of the organization's portfolio of products, services, and programs;
6. Time management instruction;
7. Use of computer technology and conservation of resources.

Please list other areas of board development or education that would be helpful to you in becoming an effective board member.

____

____

____

____

Please prioritize the following with regard to your preference for learning, with 6 as most preferred and 1 is least preferred.

_____ Case studies

_____ Training by non-staff expert

_____ Guidance from staff

_____ Articles from industry-appropriate journals

_____ Online learning modules

_____ In-person workshops located close to me

APPENDIX 5.1

Example CEO Metrics and Objectives

Please see the next page.

Performance Metrics/ Objectives	Strategic Plan (SP) Goal/ Job Description (JD) Ref.	Measurement Approach	Necessary Conditions	Weight	Threshold Performance	Target Performance	Superior Performance
Metric: Operating budget management	JD Accountability: Financial and operations	Review unaudited financial statements with Organization X Treasurer	Assumes no additional programs, services, or other items are added by the board	XX%	FY 201X actual operating income is equal to the budgeted level.	FY 201X actual operating income is 5% more than budgeted operating income	FY 201X actual operating income is 10% more than budgeted operating income
Metric: Membership growth	JD Accountability: Marketing and member services	Review Membership database	N/A	XX%	The FY 201X actual average monthly total membership level is equal to the prior year actual average monthly total membership level.	The FY 201X actual average monthly total membership level is equal to a 2% increase from the prior year actual average monthly total membership level.	The FY 201X actual average monthly total membership level is equal to a 5% increase from the prior year actual average monthly total membership level.
Metric: Membership satisfaction	JD Accountability: Member relations	Review of member satisfaction surveys	Assumes __ % return on surveys	XX%	Average satisfaction level with support provided by headquarters staff is 7 on a 10-point scale.	Average satisfaction level with support provided by headquarters staff is 8 on a 10-point scale.	Average satisfaction level with support provided by headquarters staff is 9 on a 10-point scale.

Performance Metrics/ Objectives	Strategic Plan (SP) Goal/ Job Description (JD) Ref.	Measurement Approach	Necessary Conditions	Weight	Threshold Performance	Target Performance	Superior Performance
Metric: Financial support from corporate partners	SP Goal: Increase non-dues revenue	Review unaudited financial statements pertaining to exhibit fees, advertising, sponsorships, grants, and affinity relationships.	N/A	XX%	FY 201X actual revenue from these sources is equal to the prior year actual results.	FY 201X actual revenue from these sources is equal to the budgeted level.	FY 201X actual revenue from these sources is 10% greater than the budgeted level.
Objective: Implement a new information technology platform.	JD Accountability: Infrastructure development	Review by the board of progress attained. May involve consultation with the IT director and external consultants.	Assumes the board fulfills its obligations for decision making based on approved milestones	XX%	All FY1X milestones (as approved by the board during the January 201X meeting) are attained by 1/31/1X, one month behind the projection.	All FY1X milestones (as approved by the board during the January 201X meeting) are attained by 12/31/1X.	All FY1X milestones (as approved by the board during the January 201X meeting) are attained by 10/31/1X, two months earlier than projected.

APPENDIX 5.2

Example CEO Performance Competencies

Governing Board Relations

1. Acts within role and decision-making boundaries established by the board.
2. Helps the board and individual board members operate as effectively as possible, including identification and implementation of governance best practices.
3. Builds open and constructive relations with all board members, conducive to an environment of trust and team building.
4. Demonstrates responsiveness to board members' requests for assistance and information.
5. Communicates to the board in a timely and thorough manner.
6. Ensures board agendas are complete with business plans, options for decision making, and other key information.
7. Keeps board members informed about key issues affecting the organization between board meetings.

Strategic Planning

1. Facilitates board decision making regarding which strategic plan milestones will be implemented each year.
2. Works with the board to prioritize budgetary and other resources in achieving plan milestones.
3. Ensures the organization's members and staff are appropriately engaged to implement plan milestones.
4. Keeps the board informed of milestones achieved, delayed, or deleted during the year.

5. Delivers on plan milestones as measured by the board at the end of the year.

Staff Oversight

1. Builds a high performing staff that contributes to the association's success.
2. Uses staff expertise in decision making.
3. Promotes an environment of staff customer service and responsiveness to member needs.
4. Recognizes staff for their accomplishments through compensation and recognition programs.
5. Addresses poor staff performance with appropriate progressive discipline and termination, if necessary.

Fiscal Management

1. Keeps the organization financially solvent and within budget.
2. Facilitates a thorough and timely annual budget development process, including adequate information to the board in undertaking review and approval.
3. Assures that accurate and timely financial reports are presented to the board regularly.
4. Informs the board of significant variances of actual financial performance compared to budget.
5. Ensures adequate financial policies and controls are in place.

Operations Management

1. Cultivates a mindset of continuous improvement among member leaders and staff.
2. Undertakes benchmarking and other means to identify opportunities to improve association operations.
3. Implements changes to improve effectiveness and efficiency of association operations.
4. Ensures organizational risks are identified and mitigated.

Member and External Relations

1. Develops and maintains an understanding of members' needs, expectations, and satisfaction relative to the association.
2. Maintains positive relations with the association's members.

3. Maintains positive relations with the association's corporate supporters.
4. Maintains positive relations with the association's advocacy partners.
5. Maintains positive relations with other organizations that currently or may in the future affect the association's success.
6. Represents the association effectively with governmental entities.
7. Represents the association effectively with the media and general public.

Personal Attributes

1. Displays an appropriate appearance for the position.
2. Displays energy, enthusiasm, and vigor for the position and the goals of the organization.
3. Displays fair and ethical leadership traits.

APPENDIX 5.3

Key Questions for the Incoming Chair

These questions do not need to be answered during a single meeting between the incoming chair and CEO. Ideally, the CEO has asked many of these beginning from the time the incoming chair was first identified as a rising star:

Getting to Know Each Other

- What prompted you to become a _____?
- What do you perceive to be your career highlights?
- What are you hoping to accomplish in your career going forward?
- What are your interests and hobbies outside work?
- Tell me about your family (assuming you know this is not a sore subject).
- What else should I know about you?
- What would you like to know about me?

Association Involvement

- Why did you initially decide to join our association?
- What have you appreciated most about our association?
- What do you wish were different about our association?
- What have been your most and least enjoyable roles with the association?
- What accomplishments are you most proud of in serving the association?

Current Perceptions of the Association

- What do you perceive our current core strengths to be?

- What is most concerning to you relative to the association's health and how we are serving our members?
- To what extent are you comfortable with our current strategic plan? Are there certain initiatives you would like to see us give extra priority to or, alternatively, de-emphasize during your year as chair? (Note: Any suggested changes should be vetted by the board as a whole, not just be seen as a chair's prerogative.)
- To what extent are you comfortable with our corporate and advocacy partner relationships? Are there specific relationships that you have concerns about?

Association Governance

- What do you think works well in terms of the board and committee structure and operations?
- What changes would you like to see relative to the governance structure and operations during your year as chair?
- What roles do you anticipate the various officers and other board members playing in your year as opposed to the roles they have undertaken this year?
- What changes, if any, would you like to see in the role I play during board and committee meetings?
- What topics would you like to see emphasized in the coming year during board orientation, education during board meetings, or resources available to board members between meetings?

The Chair Role

- What would constitute success for you in your role as chair this coming year? If you could look back 10 years from now, what do you hope the association will have accomplished?
- How much time do you envision devoting to your role as chair? Are certain times of the year better or worse than others given the work load of your day job and personal commitments? How can I best support you when you have the least time available for the chair role?
- What aspects of the chair role are you most excited about, and how can I help you get the most enjoyment out of these?
- What aspects of the chair role are you most concerned about, and how can I help you either handle them well or alternatively delegate them to others?

- What type of leader do you anticipate you'll be in chairing board meetings and interacting with your board colleagues between meetings? How do you think you will differ from your predecessors?
- How do you anticipate interacting with general members next year? Any changes from your predecessors?
- Do you enjoy traveling and networking/relationship building, or would you prefer to do the bare minimum in this regard? Are there certain events and locations that are more or less appealing to you (e.g., domestic versus international travel)?
- Do you have strong relationships with specific corporate or advocacy partners that I should be aware of to make sure that we leverage them to the greatest extent possible during your year as chair?
- To what extent do you feel comfortable interacting with the media? Would you like to receive media training?

Nuts and Bolts of Working Together as Chair and CEO

- What are the best days of the week/times to reach you?
- If I need to reach you on short notice, is it better to use email, phone, or text?
- Can we (staff) interact with your administrative assistant to schedule appointments? What other issues should we contact your assistant about as opposed to you?
- How often do you want to have scheduled chair/CEO update teleconferences? Weekly, biweekly, other? What day of the week and time do you prefer?
- Would you like to receive written updates of activity via email? If so, how often and in what level of detail?
- If I have concerns about a decision you're contemplating or your stance on a particular issue, what is the best/most productive way for me to convey my point of view to you?
- What other ground rules would you like to see apply to our working relationship?
- What are your reactions to ground rules I would like to propose? (Note: use this opportunity to convey your preferences about how the chair should interact with your staff, address questions or concerns, contact you outside normal business hours, etc.)

Staff-Related Issues

- What are your impressions of the headquarters staff? Do you have any specific concerns that you think I should be attuned to?
- Would you prefer me and other staff to address you by your first name or more formally? Does the answer depend on the situation (e.g., one-on-one dialogues versus group interactions)?
- How often/when would you like to visit the office and how can we make such trips productive and beneficial to you?

APPENDIX 5.4

Board Update, August 201X

Following is our performance dashboard for the first eight months of fiscal year 201X.

Metric	201X Year-to-Date (August)	201Y (Prior Year) Year-to-Date (August)
Section 1. Membership		
New Members	XXX	XXX
Active Members	X,XXX	X,XXX
Affiliate Members	XXX	XX
Associate Members	XX	XX
Student Members	XXX	XX
Senior Members	X,XXX	X,XXX
Total Members	**X,XXX**	**X,XXX**
Section 2. Annual Meeting		
Annual Meeting Registration (201X vs. 201X)	X,XXX total registrants XX% of FY1X budget	X,XXX total registrants XX% of FY1X budget
Annual Meeting Program Satisfaction (201X vs. 201X)	XX% of survey respondents would recommend the annual meeting to others	XX% of survey respondents would recommend the annual meeting to others
Section 3. Other Onsite Education		
Course A Participants	XXX	XXX
Course B Participants	XX	XX

Metric	201X Year-to-Date (August)	201Y (Prior Year) Year-to-Date (August)
Average Onsite Course Satisfaction	XX% of survey respondents would recommend the association's courses to others	XX% of survey respondents would recommend the annual meeting to others
Section 4. Online Education		
Online University Courses Participants	X,XXX	X,XXX
Average Online Course Satisfaction	XX% of survey respondents would recommend the association's courses to others	XX% of survey respondents would recommend the annual meeting to others
Abstract/Digital Poster Archive Views	XXX	XXX
Lecture Hall Views	XXX	XXX
Total Online Education Revenue	**XX% of FY1X budget**	**XX% of FY1Y budget**
Section 5. Journal		
Impact Factor (reflects prior two years content)	X.XXX	X.XXX
Journal App Downloads	XX,XXX	XX,XXX
Section 6. Corporate Support Revenue		
Annual Meeting:		
Exhibits Revenue	$XXX,XXX	$XXX,XXX
Advertising and Sponsorships	$XXX,XXX	$XXX,XXX
Educational Grants	$XXX,XXX	$XXX,XXX
Total Revenue **% of Budget**	**$XXX,XXX** **XX%**	**$XXX,XXX** **XX%**
Additional Sponsorship Revenue % of Budget	$XXX,XXX XX%	$XXX,XXX XX%
Additional Educational Grant Revenue % of Budget	$XXX,XXX XX%	$XXX,XXX XX%
Additional Publication Advertising Revenue % of Budget	$XXX,XXX XX%	$XXX,XXX XX%

Metric	201X Year-to-Date (August)	201Y (Prior Year) Year-to-Date (August)
Section 7. Website and Social Media		
Unique Visitors	XXX,XXX	XXX,XXX
Average Visit Duration	X:XX	X:XX
% New Visits	XX%	XX%
Facebook Talk About (i.e., user-initiated activity related to a page, including posting to a page's wall, "liking," commenting, sharing a page)	X,XXX	X,XXX
LinkedIn Followers	XX,XXX	XX,XXX
Twitter Followers	X,XXX	X,XXX
Section 8. Public Relations		
References in nonassociation media	Trade Publications: XX Newspapers/ Magazines: XXX Online: XXX Radio: XX TV: XX	Trade Publications: XX Newspapers/ Magazines: XXX Online: XXX Radio: XX TV: XX

APPENDIX 6.1

Corporate Partner Feedback Survey

As a valued Association X corporate partner, I would greatly appreciate your responses to the following questions. Your individual feedback will be seen only by me, although accumulated results reflecting the consensus of all survey participants will be shared with the Association X board and relevant staff. Alternatively, if you would prefer to verbally convey your feedback, feel free to contact my assistant, *name,* at *telephone number,* to arrange a mutually convenient time.

Thank you for your assistance!

Regards,
Association X CEO

. . .

	Very Well	Fairly Well	Not Very Well	Not Well at All
How well do you understand the opportunities available for you to partner with ASSOCIATION X relative to research, educational products, practice tools, sponsorships, etc.?				

What areas, if any, are unclear to you or need further explanation?

___

___

Note that the following scale response questions reference your interactions with Association X staff as a team. If you have feedback regarding specific individuals, feel free to convey those within the space provided for narrative response questions.

	Excellent	Good	Fair	Poor
How would you rate staff on managing Association X's overall working relationship with your organization?				

What additional input, if any, do you have relative to this question?

____

____

	Excellent	Good	Fair	Poor
How would you rate staff members on their ability to represent Association X (i.e., convey policies and procedures)?				

What additional input, if any, do you have relative to this question?

____

____

	Excellent	Good	Fair	Poor
How would you rate staff members on their understanding of your company's needs/priorities?				

What additional input, if any, do you have relative to this question?

____

____

	Excellent	Good	Fair	Poor
How would you rate staff members on their ability to resolve issues of conflict between your corporate needs and Association X's philosophy and operational policies?				

What additional input, if any, do you have relative to this question?

____

____

What do you perceive to be the most positive aspects in working with Association X?

____

____

How might Association X improve its interactions with you?

____

____

	Yes	No
Would you recommend support of Association X to a friend/colleague working in another company?		

If no, please indicate why not.

____

____

What additional input do you have that you believe would be helpful to Association X in improving its relationship with corporate partners?

____

____

APPENDIX 6.2

Organizational Relationships Prioritization for Association M

Priority 1 Relationships

- Association M desires to proactively partner with these organizations in achieving its mission and vision.
- These organizations are specifically acknowledged in Association M's strategic or operating plan, with defined initiatives or milestones for the relationship.
- These organizations receive annual updates from Association M of new officers and notifications of other key developments.
- Association M's board chair and CEO will proactively engage their counterparts at least once annually via teleconference or in-person meeting.
- Priority 1 relationships include:
  - Organization F
  - Organization G
  - Organization H
  - Organization I
  - Organization J
  - Organization K

Priority 2 Relationships

- These relationships are important, but not crucial, to Association M in achieving its mission and vision.
- Association M will typically respond favorably in a reactive role relative to collaboration opportunities proposed by these organizations.

- These organizations will receive annual updates from Association M of new officers and notifications of other key developments
- Priority 2 relationships include:
  - Organization L
  - Organization M
  - Organization N
  - Organization O
  - Organization P
  - Organization Q

Priority 3 Relationships

- These organizations will be on Association M's radar screen, but we typically will not devote monetary or time resources to collaborate with them, given higher priorities.
- Priority 3 relationships include:
  - Organization R
  - Organization S
  - Organization T
  - Organization U
  - Organization V
  - Organization W

Priority 1 Organizational Relationships

Organization Name	Mission/ Focus	Past/Current/Future Collaboration	CEO/Contact Information
Organization F	As identified	Description of Past Collaboration Description of Current Collaboration Description of Targeted Future Collaboration	Name Title Email: Telephone:
Organization G			
Organization H			
Organization I			

APPENDIX 8.1

Association X Risk Management Matrix

Please see the next page.

Risk Factor	Competitors	Current Status/Risk Assessment	Risk Abatement Strategy	Risk Level
PEOPLE – Board directors, other member leaders, and employees				
Board Member Liability	N/A	Association X currently maintains director and officer liability coverage through insurance broker F. Reimbursement levels vary depending on the incident.	Association X's insurance will be reviewed annually relative to coverage levels and competitive pricing.	0
Key Staff Executive Continuity	N/A	Association X does not have in force a key executive succession plan (i.e., identification of internal candidates to succeed staff officers and action steps that will be taken in the event of an unanticipated vacancy in any of these positions).	A plan pertaining to the top two executives was developed in 20XX and will be further refined in 20XX. The remainder of the executive team will be addressed in 20XX.	2
Undesirable Employee Turnover	N/A	Turnover rates for the last two years have averaged 20%, which is higher than levels experienced at similar associations.	Association X will continue to administer biannual employee engagement and opinion surveys, followed by focus groups led by an external consultant, to ensure morale levels improve.	4

Risk Factor	Competitors	Current Status/Risk Assessment	Risk Abatement Strategy	Risk Level
FINANCIAL – Membership dues, product/program/service revenue, corporate support, and investment capital and income				
Course 123	Course D, offered by Organization Y	Staff once viewed this course to be more complementary as opposed to competitive to our Course M. Course D used to focus exclusively on _____; whereas, our Course M is more comprehensive. However, the most recent version of Course D includes additional modules that serve to make it more competitive with Course M.	Staff executed a marketing plan that highlighted Course M's competitive advantage over Course D. The revision of Course 123 is underway. With the revised content, select modules are being put online. Market research was conducted in 201X to ensure content delivery meets the needs of students, providers, instructors, and directors.	4
Annual Conference	Organization F Conference	Offerings presented at the Organization F conference are of interest to our members. Continuing education credit can be earned by attending Organization F's conference. We have a collaborative relationship with Organization F and do not view the conference as significant competition to our conference.	No action at this time.	2
Advertising—Product Revenue	Various	Association X accepts advertising in publication S for products that directly compete with our own. Such advertising will continue to be allowed, given the assumption that our products are superior or, at least, perceived by our members to be superior.	The CEO will benchmark practices with other associations relative to this issue.	2

Risk Factor	Competitors	Current Status/Risk Assessment	Risk Abatement Strategy	Risk Level
GOODWILL – Overall public reputation, stature within the industry or profession, and working relationships with vendors and advocacy partners				
Corporate Satisfaction	N/A	Corporate satisfaction is partially assessed based on trends in their support levels. During the most recent fiscal year, 80% of our corporate partners maintained or exceeded their level of financial support as compared to the previous fiscal year. The previous year the corresponding percentage was 83%. Association X also measures satisfaction based on an annual survey administered to the primary contact person at each corporate partner providing more than $_____ in annual support to Association X. Ninety percent of respondents from our most recent survey indicated they were satisfied or very satisfied with the ROI they experience with our association.	We have designed a strategy for interacting with any corporate partner who decreases its support from the prior year, including personal reach-outs from the chair and CEO. This will be implemented next year. We will continue to administer annual satisfaction surveys to Gold Level corporate partners.	2
Relations with State Component Organizations	N/A	Based on the most recent annual survey, 96% of state presidents indicated they were satisfied or very satisfied with the support provided by the national headquarters office.	Association X will continue to administer annual satisfaction surveys, with the CEO proactively addressing areas of concern.	0

Risk Factor	Competitors	Current Status/Risk Assessment	Risk Abatement Strategy	Risk Level
PROPERTY – Buildings, equipment, technology, copyrights, and trademarks				
Facilities and Equipment	N/A	There is a documented business continuity plan. An insurance policy is in force with Broker M that covers Association X in the event of property loss. Reimbursement levels vary depending on the incident and the item that is damaged/destroyed. In June 20XX staff participated in a desk-top mock disaster exercise facilitated by an external consultant.	The Business Continuity Plan is a living document and is continually updated. Association X's insurance will be reviewed annually relative to coverage levels and competitive pricing. We will continue to run desk-top mock disaster exercises.	0
Online Transaction Security	N/A	Association X offers secure online ordering of products, memberships, and registrations. Our logo is prominently displayed on all web pages that have an online ordering component.	IT staff conduct ongoing monitoring of any threats to the security of online ordering.	2
Logo use	N/A	Association X is readily identified by its logo. Standards for logo display are in place. The logo standards are issued to all external entities authorized to use the logo. There has been an increase in situations where the logo has been used inappropriately on various websites and printed collateral pieces developed by other organizations.	Association X will continue to actively enforce compliance with its logo standards.	2

ABOUT THE AUTHOR

David Westman, MBA, CPA, CAE, is the chief executive officer of Westman & Associates Consulting, LLC, a firm dedicated to serving associations, foundations, certification entities, and other nonprofit organizations. Specific areas of focus include governance enhancement, strategic planning, human resources program design, project-based financial management assistance, and operational reviews.

Prior to his current role, Westman served nine years as the CEO of two international professional societies—the Emergency Nurses Association and the Congress of Neurological Surgeons. Both organizations experienced significant growth and operational improvements during his tenure. He has also served as the interim CEO for several associations, the CEO of a professional certification organization, and the CEO of several foundations that are affiliated with associations.

Earlier in his career, Westman served 15 years in leadership capacities at two large international professional service firms—KPMG and McGladrey. At McGladrey he led the Chicagoland's Strategy & Human Capital Consulting practice and served as the national Performance & Compensation Consulting Practice Champion. In these capacities at McGladrey, he doubled the size of his assigned business unit, personally sold and subsequently managed more than 100 consulting engagements, wrote numerous articles about performance improvement topics, and was a speaker at meetings of various associations.

Westman received his undergraduate degree from Augustana College (Illinois), where he was a triple major and class valedictorian. He subsequently earned an MBA in Finance and Marketing from the University of Chicago. He is both a Certified Association Executive and a Certified Public Accountant.

Westman is active in the American Society of Association Executives, where he served as chair of the Key Professional Association Committee (KPAC), consisting of 40 large association chief staff executives. He is also active in the Association Forum of Chicagoland, where he led an initiative to form a large CEO networking and best practice sharing group. In 2013 he received the Forum's Inspiring Leader of the Year award.

Outside his professional life, Westman and his wife Lori enjoy traveling and being actively engaged in the lives of their four children—Tyler, Kayla, Colin, and Derek—and their families.